INVESTING IN
YOUR INDEPENDENT
YEARS

INVESTING IN YOUR INDEPENDENT YEARS

LARRY BURKETT

VICTOR BOOKS

A DIVISION OF SCRIPTURE PRESS PUBLICATIONS INC.
USA CANADA ENGLAND

Portions of this book were adapted from *The Complete Financial Guide for Young Couples*

All Scripture quotations are from the *New American Standard Bible,* © the Lockman Foundation 1960, 1962, 1963, 1968, 1971, 1972, 1973, 1975, 1977.

Editors: Adeline Griffith, Greg Clouse, Ron Durham
Cover Designer: Joe DeLeon
Cover Photo: Comstock

Library of Congress Cataloging-in-Publication Data

Burkett, Larry.
    Investing in your independent years / by Larry Burkett.
       p.   cm.
    ISBN 1-56476-099-5
    1. Aged — Finance, Personal. 2. Investments. 3. Retirement income. I. Title.
    HG179.B838   1993
    332.024'01 — dc20   92-43091
                                                      CIP

---

1 2 3 4 5 6 7 8 9 10 Printing / Year 97 96 95 94 93

CONTENTS

INTRODUCTION

If you are over 60 you've seen some drastic changes in our economy. Inflation has become a fact of life. The years ahead will present unparalleled challenges to retirees trying to salvage their life savings from the ravages of a fluctuating economy and plodding inflation. You must determine that such uncertain financial conditions will not influence you to do less than your best in the important area of financial stewardship. You are never too old to take charge of your finances and develop sound investment strategies.

I am not an investment advisor, nor do I desire to be. A genuine concern I have is that someone might misinterpret what I say and lose some hard-earned money. If that person makes money by investing *money,* that would be bad enough; but many people I know make their money by investing their *labor.* Advising them on how to risk that money is a grave responsibility I have no desire to assume. What I will share is based on my observations as a family financial counselor. My intent is to educate, not advise.

Investing is anything but an exact science, as anyone who has ever lost money on a "sure thing" can testify. But there are basic rules that apply to investing, just as there are basic rules for physics. For example, the law of gravity says that an object will be drawn toward another object of greater mass. Thus when you jump in the air you ultimately come back down to earth. If you fill a balloon with helium, it will seemingly defeat the law of gravity, but only until the helium leaks out; then it will return to earth again.

Investing's law of risk and return works the same way. The higher the promised rate of return, the higher the risk of losing your money. Economic upturns and inflationary markets can temporarily make that law seem "defeatable," but eventually the market deflates and the high-return investments plummet to earth again, along with your hard-earned savings. So an overview of the economy reveals how it affects investment strategies.

Then a basic overview of what God's Word has to say about investing throws further light on the subject. The rules from God's Word about investing still work. Apply them and you will prosper over the long run. Violate them and you will lose all that you have worked so hard to accumulate.

Good reading, God bless you, and I trust you will decide this book has been a good investment.

1

Why Invest?

I once was challenged by a dedicated Christian who was convinced that storing assets for the future was contrary to God's will. We do have the Parable of the Rich Fool in Luke 12:16-21, which warns against storing up material goods for self while not endeavoring to be "rich toward God." But this just teaches against self-centeredness and greed, not against meeting legitimate needs.

BIBLICAL REASONS FOR INVESTING
The Bible gives several very good reasons for saving and investing, while issuing several warnings against doing so for the wrong motives.

In Praise of Industry

Solomon said, "Go to the ant, O sluggard, observe her ways and be wise, which having no chief, officer or ruler, prepares her food in the summer, and gathers her provision in the harvest" (Proverbs 6:6-8).

People who are age 60 and older are in a position to begin harvesting some of the fruits of their labors through the years. Yet they are still to keep in mind the biblical teaching about using their resources not just for their own good but for the good of others.

To Give to Others

The Parable of the Talents (Luke 19:12-26) is a clear mandate to use what God gives us—including money—in a way that earns Him a good return on His investment. The key is to be good stewards for the glory of God, and not ourselves.

The Apostle Paul directed the Corinthians to save in order to give (1 Corinthians 16:1-2). Investing wisely allows you to do this kind of giving. If the church itself is ever to break out of the borrowing habit, then Christians who invest must maintain some surpluses and be willing to give to meet legitimate needs.

Providing for Our Own

The Bible also teaches that we are to provide for our own—we who do not are "worse than unbelievers" (1 Timothy 5:8). The loving father in the Parable of the Prodigal Son obviously had a surplus that he was storing for his sons (Luke 15:11-24). And in 2 Corinthians

12:14 Paul stated an accepted doctrine in his own day that is equally true today: parents should provide for their children.

WRONG MOTIVES

Actually, in my experience not many Christians who engage in *speculative* investing do so for the right reasons. Too often lesser motives interfere.

Greed

It is very easy to rationalize greed. If you save and invest merely to gain wealth, no amount will ever be enough. For Howard Hughes, $2 billion wasn't enough. For Donald Trump, $1 billion was too little. It is important that we realize the truth of Ecclesiastes 5:10: "He who loves money will not be satisfied with money; nor he who loves abundance, with its income."

It has been my observation that those who lose the most money in investments do so because of greed. That is what motivates high-income professionals to risk money in abusive tax shelters. Most could pay their taxes and still have plenty to live on comfortably. But the desire to hang on to a little more tempts them to take excessive risks.

Slothfulness

It may seem strange to say that slothfulness is a motive for investing, but it is. Some people your age, if they failed to plan well and discipline themselves during their younger years, may be tempted to panic, and make high risk investments to make up quickly for the years they lacked foresight and industry. As Proverbs 20:4 says, "The sluggard does not plow after the autumn, so he begs during the harvest and has nothing."

Ego

Many people, Christians included, invest to bolster their pride. Why would a wealthy Texas oil family, worth somewhere between $4 and $7 billion, lose everything while trying to corner the silver market? Certainly not because they needed more money. The motive in such cases can be sheer ego and the drive to have more than others. But as Proverbs 29:23 says, "A man's pride will bring him low, but a humble spirit will obtain honor."

The Game of It

To some people, making money is simply a game, and their ego drives them to win. It can become an addiction as serious as alcohol or drugs. Everybody and everything become pawns in the game: family, friends, even God. But the wise man counsels: "Better is the poor who walks in his integrity than he who is crooked though he be rich" (Proverbs 28:6).

All this is a reminder that *we should set our financial goals and pray about them before attempting to do any investing.* If you or your spouse sense that your motives are anything but biblical, it would be better to give the money away now than risk losing something far more important than money—your soul.

BIBLICAL PRINCIPLES FOR INVESTING

There are approximately 12 basic principles of investing to be found in God's Word. Although we will be referring to most of them at one time or another, I want to lift three of them here because they address the ones most frequently violated by investors I have counseled.

Principle #1: Surety

The term "surety" means "to take on contingent liability." The most common example found in the Bible is cosigning for someone else's debts. For example, Proverbs 11:15 says, "He who is surety for a stranger will surely suffer for it, but he who hates going surety is safe."

The logic behind this warning is simple. When you cosign a note held by a third party, you have no control over when it might come due. Even cosigning for someone you know isn't safe; it's broken up many a friendship, since it's like the joke about the definition of a "distant relative"—a close relative who owes you money.

You even sign surety on your own loans when you sign a note payable and do not have a clause guaranteeing that the lender will hold you harmless if you fail to pay the loan off according to the terms of the contract. And since not many lenders will agree to such terms these days, you must be careful not to pledge too many of your assets against each new loan. This is one reason it is dangerous to invest borrowed money.

One Christian investor, whom I'll call Martin, is a sober example. He made his initial fortune in the oil and gas business in Texas and Oklahoma. Then he diversified and expanded into the blossoming real estate market. By the mid-seventies, his personal worth was said to be nearly $50 million.

Then, in 1981, the oil market collapsed, and both oil and real estate prices plummeted. Martin was sure he could ride out the crisis, but he had signed surety on every loan he acquired in recent years. When he borrowed, he pledged everything he had accumulated up to that point to secure the new loan. When many of the nation's savings and loan institutions were shut down by the government, all of Martin's outstanding loans became due and payable.

In 1990 Martin saw his home and cars being auctioned off by a court-appointed administrator. Every asset he owned—even his home—was pledged against every loan he had negotiated.

What a tragic example of the truth of Proverbs 17:18: "A man lacking in sense pledges, and becomes surety in the presence of his neighbor."

Principle #2: Risk
The general rule is: the greater the potential return on an investment, the greater the potential risk. Risk, in and of itself, is not necessarily bad. Even taking out a certificate of deposit (CD) involves some risk. After all, that's what the free market system is all about. But when the risk goes beyond common sense it is poor

stewardship, and losses become the norm.

With few exceptions, those who take excessive risks do so because they lack the knowledge or ability to evaluate the actual risk. As Proverbs 21:5 says, "The plans of the diligent lead surely to advantage, but everyone who is hasty comes surely to poverty."

Not long ago I was counseling with a couple in their late sixties who had lost their entire life savings in one of the riskiest investments possible—commodities speculation.

"Why would you take such a risk?" I asked. "Did a friend or relative talk you into it?"

"No," he replied in an apologetic voice, his head down. "I attended a one-day seminar on investing where the man said we could double our money in commodities."

"Didn't you object?" I asked his wife.

"I didn't know enough to object," she said. "I thought he was investing in some pigs since he said he was in pork bellies. And I thought soybeans would be a good investment too."

Unfortunately, this couple learned the hard way that you cannot only lose what you have, but even more than you have sometimes. The husband had opened a "margin" account to buy commodities, and lost not only their savings but owed nearly $5,000 to the exchange as well. Fortunately the broker was willing to absorb the loss and let them keep their home. Nevertheless, this husband was forced back into the sign-painting business at age 68.

Remember that risk is not the issue. Just be very certain you know what the actual risk is, and decide if you're willing and able to absorb it if there is a loss. Remember the counsel of Proverbs 27:12: "A prudent man sees evil and hides himself, the naive proceed and pay the penalty."

Principle #3: Diversification
In an ever-changing economy, no one can say with certainty what will be a good investment over the next 10 years and what will be a loser. Over the long run, there are basic areas of investing that do well. These include food, housing, transportation, and health care. But even these areas have gone through major cycles during the twentieth century. An investor who had all of his or her funds in any one area would have found it difficult to survive during a major down cycle without a large cash reserve and very little debt.

The point is, there are no sure things; so diversification is essential to long-term stability. And diversification means more than just splitting your money between stocks and bonds. It means investing in some assets that are "paper," such as stocks or bonds, and some that are real, such as real estate. It also means investing in assets that are not totally dependent on one country's economy: European stocks and bonds, Japanese companies, mortgage loans in the Eastern bloc nations, and so on.

The world's wealthiest man, King Solomon, wrote, "Divide your portion to seven, or even to eight, for you do not know what misfortune may occur on the earth" (Ecclesiastes 11:2). That advice is still as sound today as it was 3,000 years ago. As my grandfather's generation used to say, "Never put all your eggs in one basket."

2

Critical Factors

There are many strategies for investing; no one of them is better or worse than the others. In great part the strategy you select depends on your goals, your age, your income, and your temperament. Each investor must consider all of these or the result will usually be turmoil, frustration, and financial loss.

It is important to remember that good investment strategy involves a great deal more than just achieving specific goals. It involves factors such as personality and temperament, the age and stage at which you invest, and the amount of funds you want to commit.

Often our personalities and temperaments have flaws that would keep us from achieving God's full potential for our finances. To offset these flaws God, in His infinite wisdom, has given most of us spouses who mirror ourselves. In other words, they are exact opposites. I have said many times what I believe to be absolutely true: If a husband and wife are similar, one of them is unnecessary. In order to reach the proper balance in any investment strategy it is necessary that spouses communicate regularly about finances. For those who are single through choice, divorce, or a spouse's death, it is important to seek out someone close (who is as opposite as possible) to act as a counselor. One of the ways you can tell when you have found the right person is that he or she is the one individual who never agrees with you.

COMMUNICATIONS FACTOR

With some exceptions men are the primary risk-takers in the area of investments. Perhaps this is by culture, or perhaps it is by temperament, but no matter the reason it is normally so. For instance, a man often looks at a house as a potential source of capital when needed. A woman looks at a house as her home and rarely is willing to risk it unless there is no other choice.

Men are far more subject to get-rich-quick schemes than are women. In fact, of the several hundred schemes I have personally known about, less than 5 percent were promoted or purchased by women. Perhaps this is because women have been conditioned to listen rather than react, and as a result they are better able to hear the Holy Spirit's voice warning them.

This I do know: I have sat across the table from

scores of men who were describing some of the most incredibly stupid investment schemes I had ever heard of, most of which could be eliminated on the basis of common sense. Without any discussion I would often ask the wife, "What do you think about this idea?"

Her response was invariably the same. "I don't know what he's talking about, but I have a real check in my spirit about this."

With no real statistical information the wife usually came to the correct conclusion. It was as if God were saying to her, "Would you please stop this dummy before he loses any more money!"

Interestingly enough, though, if a husband is in financial need because of a bad decision and asks for his wife's help, I find most wives ready and willing to do whatever is necessary, including selling their homes, cars, jewelry, or other prized possessions.

Perhaps the Scripture verse that best describes the relationship that a husband and wife should have in all areas, including investing, is found in Genesis 2:24: "For this cause a man shall leave his father and his mother, and shall cleave to his wife; and they shall become one flesh." The closest translation to "one flesh" we have in our generation is "one person." God desires that a husband and wife function as one person, the strengths of one balancing the weaknesses of the other. One of the biggest mistakes any husband can make is to exclude his "helpmate" from the decision process. The same can be said of a wife, but for a wife to exclude her husband from financial decisions is uncommon.

Unfortunately, many wives don't want to be involved in the financial decisions of their husbands. This is very shortsighted on their part and denies the husband the balance God provides through the marriage relationship. It should also be noted that wives outlive their husbands nearly 85 percent of the time, the average age at which a woman is widowed being under 60 years of age. This means that most wives will end up inheriting their husbands' plans, whether they want to or not.

THE AGE FACTOR

Age is a very critical factor when making investment decisions. The younger you are, the more risk you can take and still recover if you're wrong. A 25-year-old investor can make some mistakes and still have plenty of time to recover. A 75-year-old investor can ill afford any mistakes, assuming he doesn't have an unlimited supply of money.

If people do not violate the principles of leverage and surety, there are virtually no situations from which they cannot not recover up to about age 40. The most they could lose is the money they have at risk. And assuming they didn't borrow it they could lose only what they have, not future earnings. Therefore, it would be reasonable for them to take more risks than someone would take at age 60 or above.

A widow, whom I'll call Betty, came in for counseling about her investment strategy. Betty's husband, Jim, had died the previous year and left her an estate consisting of $200,000 in insurance and about $150,000 in income properties. She also had their home, which was worth approximately $125,000, with a mortgage of $50,000.

Betty was 56 years old, did not desire to work, and would not be eligible for Social Security for another six years. At age 62 she would be eligible to draw approximately $600 a month in retirement benefits.

She needed approximately $1,400 a month to live comfortably. So her investment strategy had to be designed to provide her with that amount for six years (plus inflation), and then $800 a month for the rest of her life (estimated, statistically, to be 30 years).

A financial planner had recommended that she invest the life insurance in an annuity paying a guaranteed 7 percent a year for life. That would provide her with a monthly income of $1,166 for as long as she lived. In addition, with $600 a month rent from the income properties she would have a total long-term income of nearly $1,800, certainly enough to meet her needs.

On the surface, the plan she was considering was more than adequate. But I felt it had two essential flaws: First, the income properties were nearly 30 years old and required considerable maintenance. While her husband was alive he did the maintenance and leasing himself. But since she could not do the same, she was faced with an annual outlay of approximately $3,000 over the next 10 years to maintain and rent the properties. Thus her net income would be about $4,200 a year or $350 a month—a pretty poor return on an investment of $150,000 (about 2.8 percent).

The second flaw was that her annuity income was based on a single life plan. Thus, when she died, the annuity would stop. She would not be able to pass the principal or income to her children and grandchildren, a strong desire of hers. Also, since the annuity represented nearly 60 percent of her available assets, I felt that investing it in one company was too risky.

The plan we finally settled on was simple and less risky, while still accomplishing her objectives.

Step 1. She moved into one of the rental homes for three years, making it her principal residence. She then sold it for $70,000, took her one-time tax exclusion for the sale of a residence, and moved back into her original home. She used $50,000 of the proceeds to pay off her home mortgage. That was the equivalent of a 10 percent return on investment — guaranteed.

Step 2. She sold the other rental unit for about $75,000, and after taxes and tithes had approximately $60,000 left over. With the $20,000 from the first sale, she had $80,000 to invest, which she put in T-bills at 7.5 percent interest for 10 years.

Step 3. The $200,000 from the insurance was split four ways and invested in a combination of an 8 percent annuity, government bonds at 8.5 percent, tax certificates at 14 percent, and a government-backed money market fund at 9 percent.

The total income from her investments was approximately $18,500 per year. Since she paid off her mortgage she also saved $7,000 a year in payments.

The net result was to improve her income, lower her

risk, and remove the headache of rental houses. As you can see, it is possible to increase yield while lowering the risks by simple planning. In addition, since the majority of Betty's money is invested in timed deposits it can be adjusted for inflation periodically. Eventually all but the $50,000 in the annuity can be passed along to her heirs.

THE INCOME FACTOR

It seems to be a human fallacy that the more income people have at their disposal the less cautious they are with it. Some years ago I did an informal survey of some doctors and business owners I knew to determine how many of them had lost money in a bad investment. I was astounded to discover that 100 percent of those surveyed had made at least one bad investment.

Next I surveyed some middle-income families I had counseled and found out that about 50 percent of them had lost money in a bad investment.

Finally, I surveyed average-income families. Of this group about 10 percent had lost money through a bad investment.

The logical conclusion you could draw is that those in the lower income group had less money to risk so they obviously would have made fewer investments. Not so. The percentage of investments made stayed remarkably constant, regardless of the income. But the kinds of investments they chose and risks they assumed changed drastically depending on their incomes.

My conclusion is that the lower income investors are

less willing to assume high risks. The higher income investors willingly accept the greater risks. Probably much of this can be explained by what is called "sweat equity." In other words, the lower the income the more sweat went into the money to be risked.

Perhaps the lesson to be learned from this survey is: Treat all of your money as if you earned it chopping firewood for a living.

In spite of all the admonitions in God's Word against excessive risk-taking, I still receive letters from Christians who heard the truth but still violated these basic principles and lost huge amounts of money. I suppose *huge* is a relative term. If you lose all you have, it's a huge amount.

PRINCIPLE #1: GET RICH QUICK

Proverbs 23:4-5 says, "Do not weary yourself to gain wealth, cease from your consideration of it. When you set your eyes on it, it is gone. For wealth certainly makes itself wings, like an eagle that flies toward the heavens."

I have discussed the issue of "get rich quick" in other books, but I would feel remiss if I didn't cover it again, especially in a book dealing with investments. So for those who have read some of this before, forgive the repetition. For those who have not, please read carefully. This simple discussion can save you much grief and embarrassment.

It continually amazes me how gullible Christians are when it comes to get-rich-quick schemes. With rare exception, virtually all the nationwide get-rich-quick schemes begin inside Christian circles. The only logical conclusion I have been able to draw is that Christians tend to trust one another more than average non-Christians do and therefore are more easily influenced.

Perhaps one additional factor is the fact that we believe in the supernatural and will risk money in investments that require supernatural intervention. It's almost as if the more impossible the investment, the more Christians want to believe in it. This is particularly true where the promoters recite Bible verses to justify their claims.

In 1980, at the height of the Arab oil embargo, I was approached by a well-known Christian leader who told me he had been given a "revelation" from God about how to solve America's oil problems. Intrigued by his apparent sincerity, I agreed to hear his revelation. He and two other members of his leadership flew to Atlanta to present the most fantastic revelation of our generation, if it were true.

It seems that he had been approached by an angel one evening while he was praying and the angel revealed to him where the hidden oil deposits in America were located. This angel had pointed to a spot on a map where the largest oil reserves in the world lay untapped. Since it was in an area where no oil had ever been discovered previously and where the geology did not conform to any patterns established by the petroleum industry, I commented, "That would certainly explain why the oil companies have not located this vast, untapped treasure." They were looking in the "oil patch," and this was definitely not in that area.

When I asked why he felt there was oil in such an unlikely location, his response was, "Because God told me that is where it is." As far as he was concerned, that settled the issue once and for all.

"But how do you know your input is from God?" I asked.

He looked at me as if I were a heretic who had challenged the deity of Christ. "I was praying when God told me this," he said in a commanding tone.

The other two men with him nodded in agreement, certain that all my objections had been satisfied since he had received this revelation while praying. They suffered from a common delusion that prayer in itself has some supernatural meaning or power. Don't misunderstand me. I believe God can and does reveal Himself supernaturally through prayer. But the process of praying is not supernatural—God is.

"What do you need from me?" I asked, realizing further argument was useless since their minds were made up.

"We need $3 million to drill a well in this spot," the pastor replied. "It will be the biggest oil find in the world and will make us independent of imported oil. If you will endorse this project we will be able to raise the development funds."

They had already raised nearly $50,000 from people in their church to do a prospectus and brochures. But raising the rest of the money had proved very difficult.

Since I had made an absolute commitment several years before never to endorse any investment products, this helped to extricate me from an uncomfortable situation. I told them the truth, "I never endorse any financial venture. God has not gifted me to give investment advice."

I also suggested that they retain the counsel of a good securities attorney since they were offering stock in several states and it appeared to me as if they had not completed the necessary registrations.

The pastor replied that their securities registration had been blocked by Satan's forces within the state governments, and they had decided to accept money from people in those states anyway. At that point I backed away from even listening to further discussion on the subject. I believe circumstances sometimes warrant opposing government rules, but only when those rules conflict with the ordinances of God. Such would be the case if witnessing were prohibited by law, if worship of God were restricted, or if babies were being aborted. But certainly securities registration would not fall into that category.

The three men went through with the securities sale and a limited drilling operation, raising nearly $600,000 from Christians who heard about the project. In one instance a pastor from another state told his people they would be failing God if they didn't invest in this oil venture. Several families borrowed against their homes to do so. One 80-year-old couple risked their entire savings in the project.

The hole was dry and all the funds were lost, along with several pastors' credibility. Lawsuits flew like snowflakes as disgruntled Christians sued one another in violation of Paul's teachings in 1 Corinthians 6. The media picked up on the lawsuits because many elderly people had been duped into investing. As a result the cause of Christ was set back in the communities most affected. Ultimately the promoters of the venture — including the pastor — were prosecuted, convicted, and given prison sentences.

These weren't stupid people — neither the promoters nor the investors. Neither were they particularly greedy; although without a doubt, the promised returns influenced their decisions. They simply violated the basic rules that God's Word teaches on "get-rich-quick":

Don't get involved with things you don't understand.
Proverbs 24:3-4 says, "By wisdom a house is built, and by understanding it is established; and by knowledge the rooms are filled with all precious and pleasant riches."

It would be difficult to talk a geologist into an investment like the one I just described. Why? Is it because he's smarter than the average doctor who risks his hard-earned money? No, it is because he has acquired wisdom and judgment in the area of his expertise.

Don't risk money you cannot afford to lose.
Ecclesiastes 5:14 says, "When those riches were lost through a bad investment and he had fathered a son,

then there was nothing to support him." Not too long ago I risked a modest amount of money in the stock of a company that had been manufacturing computer disk drives. The company had run into some bad times due to poor management and the stock had fallen from about $20 a share to $1. I had done business with the firm several years earlier when they were the leader in the industry and I felt that perhaps under new management they could recover. So I risked $500 in their stock. I didn't want to lose the money, but I knew I could afford to.

Within one month, the company filed for bankruptcy and my stock was worthless. It was a high-risk venture, but it was not a get-rich-quick scheme. I knew the risk, could absorb the loss, and was willing to take a long-term gain.

The most common source of investment capital for get-rich-quick schemes is borrowed money. When investors risk borrowed money in anything, they are being foolish. When they borrow against their homes and needed savings (education, retirement, children), they are being stupid (in my opinion).

One pastor who invested in the oil exploration scheme I described earlier actually borrowed against his elderly mother's home to do so. That goes beyond ignorance into the realm of stupidity.

Don't make a quick decision.
Psalm 37:7 says, "Rest in the Lord and wait patiently for Him; do not fret because of him who prospers in

his way, because of the man who carries out wicked schemes." One of the prime elements of a get-rich-quick scheme is that the promoters want a quick decision. The way this is done is to make a potential investor believe that so many people want in on the deal that they're doing you a favor by giving you the opportunity first.

Usually the initial pitch is that you will get a discount or some other special consideration for getting in early. "But if you delay," the promoter warns, "the opportunity will be lost and you'll be left out."

In truth, there is an advantage in getting into most get-rich-quick schemes early on, because most of them don't survive long. So if you get in early maybe you can "sucker" enough friends in to make some money. But if you have a genuine concern for other people, you should discourage, not encourage, them to invest too.

The vast majority of get-rich-quick schemes are built on a pyramid base. This means that they require an ever-expanding supply of new investors (suckers) in order to sustain them. Usually those who join are given a monetary incentive to sell others on the scheme. If, for instance, you invest $5,000 for the right to sell synthetic oil, you can recoup your "investment" (and then some) by enticing others to do the same. These incentives are offered under the most innocuous of terms, such as "finder's fees," "royalties," and "bonuses." The bottom line is simple: If you are dumb enough to risk your hard-earned money, you must know several people who are dumber than you are.

Even as I write, new schemes are roaring through the Christian community. Some are so implausible that at first glance it's hard to believe any thinking person would respond; but they do. I have long since realized that in the realm of get-rich-quick there are no schemes too ridiculous to believe.

Most get-rich-quick schemes get started with a novel idea and enough biblical jargon to make it sound plausible within the Christian community.

Some time back, a novel get-rich-quick program surfaced in churches around the country. The premise behind this particular scheme was based on making loans without interest: a thoroughly biblical concept taught in the Old Testament. In order to participate, investors had to "contribute" 10 percent of the loan they needed. If, for instance, you needed a $50,000 loan (at no interest) you shelled out $5,000 up front — with no guarantee that you would ever get the loan.

Obviously, with no further elaboration than what I have presented, few people would be gullible enough to "invest" $5,000 with no guarantee of an eventual loan. What made this scheme work was the fact that others were receiving such loans and then telling their friends and families.

Most Christians, if they were honest, could relate similar instances when they have lost money because of trusting a Bible-spouting huckster. The "investments" range from jojoba beans in the desert to gas plasma engines that will run on water. Perhaps the most common revolutionary idea is still the 100-mile-per-gallon carburetor. Every decade or so someone will drag that one out and bilk a lot of people out of their hard-earned money. I have often wondered why the car companies would spend millions to eke out another 3 miles per gallon on new cars when they have this great carburetor sitting in the back room!

PRINCIPLE #2: WAITING TOO LONG

As I said, risk is often related to time. The principle here is very simple: People who wait too long to invest get panicky and then take excessive risks. One of the primary motivations behind state lotteries is this very mentality. Many people see the lottery as a way to make up for a lack of discipline in their earlier years. So people living on Social Security or welfare try to hit the lottery and win a million dollars (or more). The few who do are presented week in and week out as typical success stories by those promoting the system, giving false hope to those who would rather indulge now and gamble later. Obviously, what lottery promoters don't show are the millions who risk their meager earnings and lose.

PRINCIPLE #3: EXCESSIVE RISKS
THROUGH IGNORANCE

Proverbs 13:15 says, "Good understanding produces favor, but the way of the treacherous is hard." As mentioned earlier, a case can be made that everyone who takes excessive risks with their money suffers from ignorance. But we need to differentiate between doing ignorant things (like playing lotteries or trusting in a get-rich-quick scheme), and being financially ignorant.

There is no dishonor in ignorance, provided you don't choose to display it. I have absolutely no knowledge of brain surgery, nor do I desire any. So I diligently avoid all suggestions that I take a Saturday off from what I do best and perform a brain operation. That obviously sounds ridiculous, but in reality that is precisely what many brain surgeons do when they risk months, or even years, of earnings in a shopping center development with no more knowledge of that specialty than I have of brain surgery.

Recently I received a letter from an elderly couple. It seems they had retired from teaching and both elected to take their retirement savings in a lump sum, rather than take a lifetime annuity. This decision was based on the counsel of a financial planner in their church.

The annuities would have paid them a monthly income of about $600 each, which they calculated to be just barely enough to live on. Their lump sum settlement was nearly $200,000. The financial planner told them (correctly) that the lump sum could be invested safely and earn at least $1,500 a month. The additional $300 per month would mean the difference between being able to travel a little versus just paying the bills. So they took the lump sum and rolled it over into an IRA account at the savings and loan where the counselor worked. But instead of investing it in an insured account that would have been covered by the FSLIC (later the FDIC), they invested it in a bond issued by the savings and loan because it had a 2 percent higher rate of return, which amounted to nearly $300 a month more income.

Unfortunately, the S&L (savings and loan) failed and was liquidated by the FDIC within six months of the couple's retirement. The insured accounts were covered by the FDIC, and although it took some months to get all the accounts repaid, no depositors' money was lost. But the bonds issued by the S&L were not insured since they were a debt of the corporation, not the FDIC. The corporation had no assets after liquidation and consequently this couple lost their entire savings.

They took excessive risk because of their ignorance (lack of knowledge). They could have avoided this loss simply by asking any accountant, attorney, or independent financial planner what the actual risk was.

Before you risk money in any investment, first find out what the rules are. Later in this book I'll try to provide the resources you need to evaluate any given investment area.

3

Concerns At
Age 60 and Over

I f by age 60 you have achieved the financial goals you set earlier in life, basically you need to concentrate on preserving what you have worked so hard to accumulate.

Obviously if you have not achieved your goals, you will need to delay your retirement plans and work to become debt-free, accumulate the supplemental funds you and your spouse will need, and adopt a very conservative lifestyle. It is unfortunate that so few Americans establish any realistic financial goals early in life and face the 60-plus years with unrealistic expectations.

The most common mistake most Americans make is to retire without adequate financial preparation. They simply believe that 62 or 65 represents the "mandatory" retirement age, regardless of their situation. Two points need to be made here: First, there is no mandatory retirement age (not biblically). Many people can and do remain gainfully employed long into their seventies and even eighties. Perhaps they cannot work as hard, but they have learned to work a lot smarter.

Second, you cannot take a 50 percent (or more) cut in income and expect to enjoy your retirement years. Unless you have adjusted to the projected retirement income level at least three years prior to retirement, you're fooling yourself.

Often those who retire without adequate preparation find themselves trying to reenter the job market shortly after retiring only to find that they can't earn anywhere near the salary level they left. Many end up taking entry-level jobs at very low wages. They would have been far better off to have stayed at the job they left. Current laws prohibit mandatory retirement, except in age-critical professions, such as airline pilot. So retirement is an option, not a requirement.

Let me restate an absolute. If you can't adjust to the projected income you expect to receive after retirement at least three years before that time, stay where you are! Reset your retirement goals to 65, 68, or 80, but don't become a poverty statistic. As Christ said in Luke 14:28-30:

> For which one of you, when he wants to build a tower, does not first sit down and calculate the cost, to see if

> he has enough to complete it? Otherwise, when he has laid a foundation, and is not able to finish, all who observe it begin to ridicule him, saying, "This man began to build and was not able to finish."

I saw an interesting example of this principle at work a few years back. Phil and Andy, both in their sixties, worked for a wholesale automobile supply company. Andy, the delivery man (called an expeditor), earned about $12,000 a year. Phil, the plant manager, earned about $40,000 a year. Neither had put any significant savings aside, nor had either taken advantage of the company's retirement plan. Phil, the plant manager, obviously lived in a bigger home, drove better cars, and took better vacations during his working career.

At age 62 each elected to take an early retirement option from the company. Andy received a lump sum of about $10,000 from the company; Phil received a lump sum of about $35,000.

By coincidence both men came in for counseling about two years after retirement. Andy had adjusted very well to his Social Security income, in addition to working a part-time delivery job that paid him about $50 a week. In fact, Andy and his wife were actually better off financially than when he had been fully employed. All they needed was some budgeting help to maintain better control of some nonmonthly expenses, such as annual insurance, home taxes, and car repairs.

Phil, on the other hand, was in deep financial trouble. He had spent all of his severance bonus and had run up sizable credit card debts. The reason was obvious. He had taken more than a 50 percent cut in income to retire on Social Security alone. The severance bonus buffered him for a little more than a year, but when it ran out his lifestyle crashed in on him. Phil attempted to find work also but could locate only minimum wage jobs.

In reality Andy, the delivery man, was better prepared than his boss. He made nearly a lateral move into retirement because he never had the money to indulge or to accumulate any debt to speak of. Phil took a drastic income reduction and was unable to make the adjustment. The principle is taught clearly in Proverbs 12:9, "Better is he who is lightly esteemed and has a servant, than he who honors himself and lacks bread."

ALTERNATE INCOME

Before discussing financial strategy for those 60 and older I would like to share an observation: A marketable skill is the most dependable retirement plan anyone can have. As long as you are reasonably healthy, you will never be listed among the impoverished in our society.

This idea is neither new nor original with me. It is a concept that was traditional until the last two generations. Most young men learned a trade while they were at home. Even if they left that trade and went to college or into another business, the skill was still retained. I used this approach to work my way through college long before any banker was crazy enough to lend a college student money.

When I was in high school I knew that my family would not be able financially to help me go to college. So for several summers in high school I worked as an apprentice electrician and attended night classes twice a week to pass the journeyman electrician's license test. By the time I finished high school I had my license and was earning about $3 an hour, while my friends who worked in grocery stores or retail stores were making $1.25 an hour. That trade allowed me to work my way through college at the Cape Canaveral Space Center in Florida, eventually becoming a manager of an experiments station. Although I have not worked at the trade for nearly 25 years now, I still remember the fundamentals and could market that skill to earn a living if necessary.

Anyone approaching retirement who has doubts about having enough income can do the same thing. Just sign up for night classes at any good vocational school and learn a trade that suits your abilities; you'll always have an income. If you don't believe it, just try to hire someone to check out your air conditioner (or fix a faucet, or build a closet, or paint your house) and see what it costs.

RETIREMENT STRATEGY

For those who have met their goals—they are debt-free and have enough investment savings for the winter years—it's time to start making some adjustments in strategy. The basic strategy for over age 60 is to develop a more conservative long-range outlook. The principal objective now becomes one of protection and conservation, rather than growth.

That does not mean to shift all of your assets into U.S. Treasury bills. Your strategy may be as simple as shifting from high-growth mutual funds to income funds. Usually any mutual fund company offers a wide range of investment pools or mixes, each with a differing objective. By requesting a prospectus, any investor can determine which of the plans best fits the age and strategy needed.

I have chosen to use a tiered system to describe the types of investments used at this stage of life. You will notice a decided shift toward the conservative end of the tier at this point. It doesn't matter whether you elect to use mutual funds, stocks, real estate, or collectibles to build your investment base; you still need to shift strategies with enough of your assets to secure the income you need to live on.

By adopting this more conservative strategy, you will probably miss out on some of the major stock market rallies, as well as some of the better "deals" offered by your brother-in-law who just went to work for the plasma engine dealer. Such is life. If you want to retire with some degree of financial security you will need to make such sacrifices. The whole object from age 60 on is to try to avoid the disasters that can wipe you out totally.

If, after securing the major portion of your assets,

you still have funds with which to speculate, that is a decision between you, your spouse, and the Lord.

Remember that the one variable in this age-related strategy is inflation. If inflation is re-ignited by the massive debt spending of our government, you will need to adjust your planning. Inflation can erode your long-term assets just as surely as a bad investment can.

THE TIERED SHIFT

Let's assume that you are approaching 60-plus and have achieved most of your goals through the use of mutual funds and rental real estate. Now you need to make the necessary adjustments to a more conservative posture. The following illustration shows how your funds could have been allocated up to this point. The majority (nearly 80 percent) of the investments were oriented toward some aggressive funds during your forties and fifties. The only funds left in the most conservative tier were those used to pay the bills for your children's college education as they came due.

Now the shift to the conservative side is necessary. About six months salary will be maintained in a cash reserve account to meet emergencies. As the regular dividend income is received, it is deposited in this account. Once the account accumulates more than eight months reserve, it is shifted to a longer term cash reserve account, such as a CD, to earn more interest.

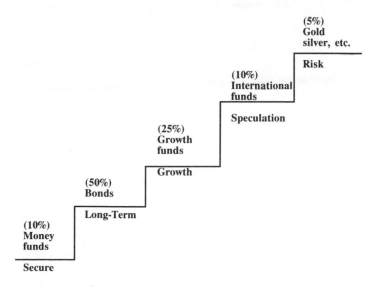

The goal is to maintain a spendable income of approximately $2,500 per month at retirement — including Social Security, investment earnings, and some generated income.

One additional note here: Since earned income can affect your Social Security pension, it is critical to shift as much of the earned income as possible to unearned income. There are several ways to do this. It should be noted that the tax laws change frequently so these options may or may not be available at the time of your retirement. However, the one certainty is that some options will always be available, since our elected officials also retire.

USING A CORPORATION

If you have earned income and can shelter it within a corporate structure, you can avoid some of the earned-income liability. The corporation can provide medical, life, and disability insurance without affecting your Social Security income. It also can retain the earnings or profits and redistribute them as dividends. Obviously, there would be some additional tax considerations. But if the amount of corporate income taxes paid are less than the loss of Social Security due to earned income, you will still benefit.

Also a corporation can offer you a Section 125 plan (often called a Cafeteria Plan) where 100 percent of your salary can be assigned. From this plan you can pay all medical expenses, child care for dependents, dental, eye care, etc. This does not affect your Social Security earnings and is exempt from all taxes.

Before using a corporation to shelter income, it is essential that you consult a good tax accountant. Tax laws do change frequently and only a working professional in the field can advise you properly.

I will use the example of a Christian I'll call Don to demonstrate what can be done with some good planning.

Don was a computer specialist with a large company and elected to accept their early retirement plan at age 62, even though he had not planned to leave the company for several more years. The early retirement package, including a lump sum settlement, actually provided him with more than the amount he would have earned during the following five years, had he continued to work.

Don had a specific retirement goal: He desired to do volunteer mission work with his church six months of the year and operate a computer consulting company the other six months.

He invested the majority of the lump-sum settlement in conservative bonds and other securities. This provided him with a monthly income of approximately $2,000. In addition, his Social Security provided another $1,200 per month. This amount would have been higher except that Don had been exempt from the system for 10 years earlier in his life.

Don and his wife lived in an extremely high-cost area of the country and desired to remain there as long as possible to work with their church and stay close to their children and grandchildren. In order to do so,

Don required an additional $600 per month. So he established a corporation through which he would do his consulting. The company provided him with a supplemental health care plan for Medicare, a company vehicle, and a Section 125 plan to pay for all additional health related expenses, thus dropping his total monthly expenses by nearly $400. Once a year Don would also receive a dividend check from the company, providing the remaining income he required (on which he had to pay income taxes). Since the dividend was not earned income, his Social Security benefits were not affected.

As the company accumulated retained earnings, Don used some of the funds for the ministry he was involved in, as well as for a cash reserve in times of emergency.

In a matter of months Don had shifted his strategy from a retirement age of 67 to 62 with no reduction in annual income. By January of the next year he and his wife were doing mission work in Central America, helping to evangelize business people in that area—a goal he had established as a part of his strategy nearly 10 years earlier.

CATCHING THE VISION

I trust that by now you have correctly assessed the rationale behind planning for this stage of your life. It will free you to continue to be active and serve others without the pressures of earning and accumulating the needed funds through daily labor.

Therefore, retirement is not what most Americans think of as the time to stop all gainful employment. Rather, it is the time to shift into a higher gear, free from the pressures of the competitive work world to a large degree. If, for some reason, the Lord allows the entire U.S. economy to fail, including many of our own investments, we will have the assurance of knowing that we were the best possible stewards of the resources He gave us to manage. The worst that can happen to us is to lose some or all of our surpluses and continue to work at whatever level we are capable. Being debt-free makes that strategy a lot more feasible.

One closing thought on the concept of staying active: Several recent studies have shown that many men and women once thought to suffer from irreversible senility recovered much of their earlier abilities by daily exposure to mental and physical stimulation. Some studies even indicated that active older people experience a regeneration of brain activity, once thought to be impossible. It is not surprising that the scientific community is beginning to discover what we Christians already knew: God created us to be productive beings throughout our entire lifespan. As the old cliché goes: "Use it or lose it."

4

The Worst Investments

I t's important to note that this chapter deals more with observations than it does with scientific studies. By that I mean I am offering a counselor's view of investments I have seen others make that have consistently lost money. Obviously, there are investment advisors who will disagree with my observations. That's okay too, because I would probably disagree with theirs. The criterion I use here is very simple: Of the people I have known and counseled over the years, which investments made them money and which lost?

Perhaps the simplest, most straightforward method for evaluating any investment is the percentage of people who buy into it and get their money back. The next rule of thumb is how many made a return above their investment. It's very much like evaluating your financial advisor. The rule of thumb is: If he makes you more money than he costs you, he's pretty good.

I have purposely oriented this book toward nonprofessional investors like myself. Even though I am a financial counselor and teacher, I am not a professional investment advisor. The difference between being a counselor and a professional investment advisor is that I don't risk other people's money.

I have always tried to limit my advice to basic financial areas such as budgets, financial goals, and biblical principles. I would personally find it rather hard to sleep at night knowing that I had the responsibility of overseeing the management of other people's money.

Most successful investors are what I call *hedged risk-takers.* By that I mean that they will take risks periodically if they can afford to, but they never take more risks than are considered necessary to accomplish their goals. There are investments that potentially can return great financial rewards, but most are what should be called "sucker bets." (Forgive my use of gambling terms, but that's what most of these are.)

Amateur investors who attempt to beat the odds on high-risk investments do nothing but feed more money into the pockets of the professionals. The brokers on the commodities and stock exchanges make money whether the investors do or not. They make it when their clients buy and then again when they sell. It matters naught whether the investors make or lose money on the transactions (as far as commissions are concerned). It would be great if a brokerage house would agree to forgo all commissions if the products they sell don't return a profit, but it doesn't work that way.

Over the years I have seen some very good investments and some very bad ones. It is impossible to categorize any single investment absolutely. Someone with specialized abilities can take a risky investment and make it less risky because of his or her knowledge and ability. As it is throughout this book, my analysis of risk is based on the average, nonprofessional investor. If you are a thoroughly professional investor and average 25 percent a year return on your capital, you probably wasted some of it on this book. If you think you are a professional investor and average less than 25 percent a year return, you're probably fooling yourself, so read on.

WORST INVESTMENT #1:
COMMODITIES SPECULATION

Commodities trading is the buying and selling of materials for future delivery. Perhaps the best book ever written on this subject for the average investor is *God in the Pits* by Mark Ritchie, a professional commodities trader in Chicago. Mark is a Christian and a good friend, and is clearly one of the most successful commodities traders in America.

In chapter 1 of his book Mark describes the details of how the Hunt fortune was lost through speculative trading in the silver futures market. That one story should be frightening enough to convince any novice with less than $5 billion that commodities trading is not for the sane investor.

I have known Mark for many years, so I think I understand the mentality of what it takes to be a Christian in the commodities business. Unless you have the absolute conviction that everything you own belongs to God (literally) and can go to bed at night with the understanding that everything you have worked for most of your life can be lost while you sleep, don't trade commodities.

In the past several years, as the commodities business has become less attractive to the average investor, many speculators have shifted to trading in option contracts. An option contract gives an investor the right to purchase a futures contract at a future date. If that doesn't confuse you, nothing will.

Basically, it means that, as an investor, you pay a fee for the right to buy a contract at a future date. If the material goes up while you hold the option, you may elect to exercise the option and purchase the contract. More commonly, the option itself is resold at a profit.

The other side of options is that if prices decline you can elect to drop the option, forfeiting the option money. The advantage of options, as opposed to an actual futures contract, is that the downside risk is the amount you have paid for the option. In a futures contract the risk is potentially much greater.

Allow me to illustrate. Let's assume you purchase a futures contract to deliver soybeans in 90 days at $5 per bushel, and they are presently selling for $4 a bushel. A smart investor would buy a contract for 1,000 bushels to be delivered in 90 days at $5, and immediately purchase 1,000 bushels at market price for $4. You just made $1,000 and all you have to do is store the beans for 90 days; it's a good deal. But what if in three months soybeans are down to $3 a bushel? In that case you will have just lost $1,000.

The losses can be greatly magnified through credit. Suppose you bought the contract on margin (credit) and put down 50 percent. If soybeans go to $5 a bushel, you stand to make more than 300 percent in 90 days. If they go to $3, you can lose the same percentage! The risk is high, but so are the potential profits. If they weren't, who would be foolish enough to risk money?

Commodities trading does have an honorable purpose, though it has been lost in the mad dash for instant riches. The commodities exchange was created to provide a method for farmers to presell their crops, thus assuring them a variable, but guaranteed, price each season. However, a quick check of the volume traded on the commodities exchange reveals that many more future delivery contracts are sold than crops are grown. What that obviously means is that many commodities contracts are never meant for delivery. They are paper transactions, designed and used only for speculation.

Trying to guess the future prices of agricultural commodities can be a stressful way to earn a living. I recall when the fighting between England and Argentina erupted over the Falkland Islands several years ago, the common logic was that soybean prices would skyrocket since Argentina was a major producer of that commodity. But, contrary to logic, after the English launched their attack the price of soybeans went down limit (the maximum allowed by the exchange in a single day's trading). Those speculators who guessed wrong, including my friend Mark, found themselves unable to sell their contracts. That's known as "catching a financial alligator." They're a lot easier to catch than to let go. Mark suffered his losses and survived, but I'm sure there were many others who lost a lifetime of earnings.

When the Gulf War broke out in January 1991 the same anomaly happened with oil. The common consensus was that oil prices would skyrocket to around $40 per barrel. Those who purchased future delivery contracts at the prevailing $26-per-barrel rate at the outbreak of the war saw prices plummet to nearly $20. That's called "wipe out."

There are ways to reduce the overall risk in commodities, such as buying options. But even so, this merely limits the downside risk. It does not reduce the risk of losing your investment money. My advice to anyone who does not own a seat on the Chicago Board of Trade is: Stay out of the commodities business. And to those who do own seats on the board—sell them and get an honest job.

WORST INVESTMENT #2:
PARTNERSHIPS

Contrary to some teachers in Christian circles, I do not believe the Bible prohibits Christians from being in partnerships. The admonition against partnerships with nonbelievers in 2 Corinthians 6:14-15 is clear but does not extend beyond that.

Having made the point that partnerships between believers are allowable, in no way do I mean to imply that they are advisable—especially financial partnerships.

The Apostle Paul wrote to the Corinthians that "all things are lawful for me, but not all things are profitable" (1 Corinthians 6:12). That is a very good principle to bear in mind. The Lord told Peter that he should "kill and eat" (Acts 10:13). The instructions were clear that all foods and animals were allowable to eat. I would assume that would include buzzards and skunks, but they wouldn't be too palatable.

In the investment arena the most common financial partnerships are "limited partnerships," meaning that the contractual arrangement specifies a "general" or managing partner, and one or more nonmanaging or "limited" partners. The intent of a limited partnership is to limit the liability of the nonmanaging partners to their financial investments only. Thus they would be sheltered from lawsuits, contract defaults, and future losses.

Based on observation I have often wondered if the "limited" in limited partnerships means that a participant is limited in his or her ability to get back the money invested. Some limited partnerships require future financial participation in the event of operating losses or specified capital infusions, so they aren't all that limited. But even the limited partnerships that specify no future financial obligations have one hidden flaw — recapture.

Recapture is a nasty rule practiced by the IRS that says: When a property is sold or foreclosed, some or all of the previous tax deferments become due and payable, and the forfeiture of any outstanding debt becomes "phantom" income. The income may be "phantom," but the taxes aren't. They are due and payable when the loan is transferred back to the lender.

Understanding tax deferment is crucial when investing in any partnership that provides a tax write-off. There are virtually no tax eliminations where the IRS is concerned. True tax eliminations are things like tax credits, personal exemptions, operating losses, and such. All other tax reductions are called deferments, meaning that they are delayed until the investments are sold or otherwise transferred. It's the "otherwise" that has gotten many unknowledgeable investors into trouble.

Allow me to share a typical horror story involving a limited partnership. A Christian I'll call Henry developed some limited partnerships to invest in apartment complexes. He was particularly good at taking complexes that were losing money and turning them around. The limited partners were required to invest enough money to renovate the complexes and provide enough operating capital to carry the complexes until they could be rented. There was nothing wrong with Henry's investment philosophy and, based on an estimated five-year holding period before the complexes were resold, the average return to the investors was over 50 percent a year! With that kind of return there was no lack of willing investors.

Some of the complexes were particularly desirable income properties. These were kept for income rather than sold. As the properties appreciated in value, the general partner, Henry, borrowed the original investment capital (and then some) out of the complexes and returned it to the partners. Effectively the investors had an appreciating asset that generated good income in which they had virtually no money. That's a good deal by any investment standard.

When a complex was sold the partners knew they would have capital gains taxes to pay as well as some recapture of depreciation write-offs, depending on how long the complex had been held. Since they made a sizable profit from the sale, it was no difficulty to pay the taxes. But an event occurred that was ultimately to shatter the bubble of high returns with low risk.

In 1986 President Ronald Reagan proposed the most sweeping changes in the tax laws since the late sixties. One of the changes was to disallow tax write-offs from passive income investments (such as apartment complexes) against earned income. This meant that many high-income investors who bought properties and used the depreciation to shelter their regular income lost that capability. The result was an almost instant collapse of limited partnerships in general, and income property partnerships in particular. Basically there were virtually no buyers for apartment complexes that were developed to shelter taxes.

Even worse, new complexes under construction were dumped on the market at drastic discounts. Investors backed out of many new complexes and desperate mortgage lenders hired managers to rent them out at far below the going market rates. Complexes that had previously been profitable suddenly became money losers.

Many of Henry's complexes fell into arrears and were foreclosed by the lenders. Each complex that was foreclosed carried with it a tax liability for the accumulated depreciation and forgiveness of debt. The outstanding debt was considered as income to the partners when the mortgage companies reassumed the liability. The partners found themselves faced with hundreds of thousands of dollars in tax liabilities and no money to pay them.

Many limited partners, whom I know personally, will be repaying their taxes for several years at substantial interest rates. Their homes are attached as collateral and several have had their personal assets sold at public auction. Their liability was not as limited as they had been led to believe.

WORST INVESTMENT #3:
TAX SHELTERS

Although this category includes some of the other all-time worst investments, such as the limited partnerships just described, I decided to list it separately because it is a great way to lose everything you have and then some.

Tax shelter investments are in a category by themselves simply because they are used primarily to defer income taxes rather than for any economic value they might have. It does not mean that they have no economic value. Any investment that has no economic value is prohibited, according to tax law. But if the intent is primarily the deferment of current tax liability, then I would classify that investment as a tax shelter.

Since the 1986 Tax Reform Act, tax shelters for the average investor have been much curtailed. As noted earlier, passive investment tax benefits cannot be used to shelter earned income (in most cases). Therefore, it is usually the investor with significant passive income who is attracted to existing tax shelters.

But since all things that go around come around, tax shelters for the average investor will return; of that I have no doubt. In the meantime, there are still sufficient numbers of shelters being peddled to attract the gullible.

As you might guess, I am somewhat negative about tax shelters as investments. The reason is simple enough: I have known many fine people who have lost virtually everything they owned as a result of them. About the only people who have regularly made money from tax shelters are the salespeople, attorneys, and accountants.

Tax shelter investments prey on the uninformed and the greedy (my opinion). The simple truth is that unless you are willing to spend years in court and lots of money on accountants and attorneys, you will not beat the IRS at their own game for two basic reasons. One, they can use your own money to fight you. Two, they have the ability to change the rules in the middle of the game.

I can think of a hundred personal examples of people I have known who thought they could "beat the system." But in the interest of time and space I will share only one.

A Christian professional athlete whom I'll call Bob was being counseled by a "Christian" investment advisor on how best to maximize his income during his professional career. Bob was a fairly typical pro football player—though intelligent and skilled at his sport, he had practically no business experience. His salary of nearly $200,000 a year seemed enormous when compared to the pittance he and his wife had been living on in college. But after paying his taxes, tithes, normal living expenses, and additional in-season living expenses, he had less than $10,000 a year left over to invest.

Unfortunately for Bob, his investment advisor followed a strategy of using multiple tax shelters to save as much tax as possible and then using the tax money to invest for the future.

He put Bob into a Brazilian opal mine that would shelter $10 in taxes for every $1 invested (using leveraged notes payable). Next he suggested Treasury bill straddles (if you don't know what these are you're better off). These provided an artificial loss at the end of each tax year. Finally, he put Bob into a highly leveraged equipment leasing deal that would shelter nearly $20 in taxes for every $1 invested (again using future debt and investment tax credits).

The result was that Bob saved all of his tax liability (federal and state). This provided him with an additional $70,000 a year to invest (less the $30,000 it took to invest in the tax shelters). Bob was convinced that his advisor was a wizard.

The advisor then helped Bob invest in several real estate and business deals for which the advisor received a commission. He also had received either commissions or finder's fees for placing Bob in the tax shelters. I always thought it interesting that during this time the advisor did not invest in any of these tax shelters himself, although he did risk some money in the more traditional investments.

Bob retired from professional football in 1984, expecting to be able to live off of his investments and whatever income he could earn as a teacher and coach. Instead he got the biggest shock of his life: a letter from the IRS stating that he was being audited.

The audit quickly progressed from bad to nasty, with the agent recommending that the IRS disallow all of the tax shelters. He further recommended that 50 percent penalties be assessed, along with interest.

Bob quickly hired a tax attorney to represent him before the IRS. After investigating the shelters, the attorney recommended that Bob plead for mercy. It seems that in the case of the T-bill straddles the investment company hadn't even bothered to make the trades each year. They just sent a falsified report to Bob's accountant. Even if they had made the trades the IRS would have disallowed the deduction as a sham transaction, but in this case there was no defense — not even ignorance.

When the dust settled, Bob owed more than $200,000 in taxes, interest, and penalties, with the interest clock continuing to tick.

Unfortunately, Bob's money was gone by then. He couldn't get his investment money back, and the tax shelter companies had folded and fled into the night. Bob lost his home, cars, investments, and even had his retirement account with the NFL attached for taxes. He now works a full-time job, with the IRS receiving nearly one fourth of his total take-home pay.

WORST INVESTMENT #4:
PRECIOUS METALS

I know I'm going to irritate some friends who believe in precious metals as investments. But I have to say what I believe and, thus far, most of the people I know who have made money on precious metals are those who sell them.

There are two basic reasons why people invest in precious metals such as gold and silver. The first, as with any other commodity, is to speculate on their rise and fall. The second is as a hedge against a future collapse of the economy and/or the currency system.

One negative aspect of speculating in precious metals is the cost of buying and selling them. Unlike stocks and bonds, which have a well-organized and highly competitive market, precious metals have no such market. Investors can buy contracts for future delivery of precious metals in the commodities exchange, just as for virtually any commodity, but buying the actual metal is limited to a relatively few traders around the country.

These traders or dealers mark up the metals, usually from 5 to as much as 12 percent, when they sell them. Then when they repurchase the metals they make an additional premium by way of a discount from the quoted retail price. Essentially investors buy at retail and resell at wholesale. It takes a significant rise in price to make up the fees.

I know there are individual exceptions to this rule, but discount brokers and buyers are not available to the average precious metal investor.

In the case where an investor is buying precious metals as a hedge against a potential economic disaster, there is some justification for not listing them among the "worst" investments. After all, we haven't had a real depression since the thirties, so we don't know how metals will fare. So in fairness to those who sell gold and silver as a hedge against a collapse, I will downgrade my evaluation to merely a "questionable" investment.

Those who bought gold at $30 an ounce and saw it climb to over $500 an ounce in the seventies would probably disagree. But again, for the average investor who bought in after that one spectacular event, the trend has been level — to down.

Even the most enthusiastic precious metals advocates rarely defend the purchase of silver anymore. So many novice investors got wiped out in the great fall of silver in the early eighties that most dealers speak of silver in whispers only. In reality the depressed price of silver probably makes it one of the better speculative risks for the next decade.

The difficulty with buying precious metals (primarily gold) as a hedge against collapse is one of determining the future of gold as a currency. Traditional hard money advocates say that when a nation's (or world's) currency gets too inflated it will collapse and people will return to the gold standard. Unfortunately, that theory was developed before the communications age we are in today. It is my strongly held conviction that the next currency will be neither gold nor paper. It will be electronic transfers, regulated and controlled by a central world bank.

If that proves to be true, and only time will tell, gold will be little more than a speculative commodity again. Those who don't believe this could happen need to read the arguments from the thirties that the United States could not remove its currency from the gold standard. We did it because of the desire to put out massive amounts of paper money without the requirement to collateralize it with gold. The same mentality (political necessity) may well divorce all world currencies from the confinements of a limited supply of gold. I am not advocating this reasoning. I am simply looking at the facts and stating my opinion.

WORST INVESTMENT #5:
GEMSTONES

A woman may well treasure the diamond she wears on her finger or around her neck, but it is not an investment. For the average investor the same can be said of most precious and semiprecious gemstones. Most novice gem speculators usually buy high and sell low.

Several factors encourage me to list gems in my worst investment category, not the least of which is the difficulty for the average investor to tell the quality and value of gems.

There are grading organizations that will swear to a gem's quality, clarity, and estimated value. But unless you can resell to the same dealer that sold the stone to you, the next trader may not accept the evaluation. Even if the original dealer does agree to repurchase the gem(s), there is no guarantee you will get the current market value. The market value of gems is nebulous at best, and is not quoted daily as are company stocks.

In the mid-seventies several large traders pooled their resources in an attempt to create a ready market for precious gems, particularly diamonds. Unfortunately, all that came of it was a dramatic increase in the price of diamonds as the companies marketed them aggressively. Many individuals bought "investment grade" diamonds after being assured they were secure investments. "After all," the salesmen said, "diamonds have held their value better than any other investment over the last 100 years." This was true to a large extent because the DeBeers trading company of South Africa controlled the supply of diamonds very carefully, allowing only a few investment quality stones on the market each year.

The net result of this debacle can best be demonstrated by a gift a supporter made to our ministry a few years back. He bought a one-carat "investment" quality diamond in 1982 for approximately $16,000. It was sealed in a plastic container along with a certificate issued by a certified appraiser.

In 1986 he donated the diamond to our ministry. We attempted to sell it at what was estimated to be its fair market value of nearly $20,000 (based on the opinion of the original dealer). Two prospective buyers sent the stone to be reappraised. The first appraisal downgraded the stone's quality one full point, lowering the value to about $9,000. The second came back two points down, with a value of $5,000. There were no buyers at either price, I might add.

I told the shocked donor, who immediately went to the dealer who sold him the stone. He had a written option to resell the diamond to the dealer at the original sales price at any time. The dealer told him a sad tale about his misfortune with other investors and notified him that he had filed for bankruptcy.

Over the last 20 years or so I have counseled many

people who have purchased gems as investments. Some were happy because the gems were safely locked away in their safety deposit vaults appreciating greatly, according to the reports they received annually from their dealer/broker. And I am quite sure that many investors who resell their gems to friends and family do make a profit. But to date I have not met a single novice (nonprofessional) investor who has made money on gems, except by reselling to another friend who didn't know better either.

WORST INVESTMENT #6:
COINS

Collectible coins, stamps, and other unique items can be good investments for knowledgeable buyers who take the time and effort to become proficient at their trade. It is not to this group that I speak. Nor is it to those who collect coins and stamps for a hobby. Basically they don't care if the items appreciate or not. Obviously anyone would rather their assets appreciate, but if they are not going to sell them, who cares?

I restore old cars as a hobby, and I really don't intend to sell them. I periodically check to see what equivalent cars are selling for but only by way of interest. Most of the cars have so much of my labor in them that at double the market price I would net about a dollar an hour for my time. For me, it's a hobby, not an investment.

Several companies offer numismatic (collectible) coins as investments. In the eighties collectible coins became very popular investments, not only because they could appreciate in value as collectibles but also because the coins usually contained precious metals.

There is no doubt that many numismatic coins have appreciated over the last two decades, so why list them among the worst investments? Because, in general, it is the professional collector who has done well, not the novice investor. In recent years many trade shows have developed to buy and sell coins. These establish a market for coins and have helped to standardize the pricing through a very detailed grading system between traders.

But if the market for collectible coins were limited to dealers only, the prices would quickly settle down with little or no appreciation. Why? Because the traders would all know the true value of the coins and would not sell too low or buy too high (except for extreme cases of hardship).

For the price spiral to continue, it is necessary to market the coins to the general public. Thus a trader buys coins at their true market value at a show, then resells them to investors (usually through a recruited mailing list) at higher prices. If enough investors can be found, the dealer makes his own market.

If a novice investor attempts to resell a coin at the listed market price, he quickly discovers that what he paid was retail and the price he is offered is wholesale. The dealer buys low and sells high, so the investor is forced to resell to the dealer at a substantial discount.

If dealers would make their mailing lists available

(which they won't), investors might be able to command dealer prices. Some dealers will offer to resell your coins or even repurchase them at the wholesale price. But unless the coins have appreciated greatly, you end up either losing some of your investment or, at best, making a small gain. Again, drawing on the testimonies of many people I have counseled who purchased coins for investment purposes, the vast majority said they lost money; some of them, a lot of money!

If you're not interested in studying numismatic coins, you'll probably find they are not a good investment for you. One side note is necessary here. If you ask friends who bought coins, they will probably tell you they did well. That's because, compared to some of the other investments they made, the coins lost the least. That is not exactly what you're looking for from your investments.

WORST INVESTMENT #7:
STOCKS

Since I have already alienated a large number of my friends who sell investments, I figure that I might as well go the whole way and irritate the rest — so I have included stocks among my worst investments list.

Again, I would emphasize that a knowledgeable, professional investor can and does make money regularly on common stocks. Also, anyone can learn how to evaluate stocks and reduce the risks involved. But for the average investor, today's market is not like that of our fathers' day. Determining which stocks will do well and which will not is a highly technical field that very few investors are equipped to handle.

I would also like to make it clear that I am not trying to discourage those who invest in a single stock, such as that offered by the company they work for. I am referring to novice investors who buy stocks based on their "gut" feelings. More often than not, what they are feeling are simple gas pains.

If you took a portion of your savings and bought a representative sample of "blue chip" stocks and then just held onto them for 20 years, you would do fairly well. From 1970 to 1990 your investment would have kept pace with inflation and earned about 3 percent a year in real growth. Unfortunately, the average investor doesn't do that. He hears of a strong bull market and jumps in, trying to make a big hit. Usually by the time he hears about the bull market it has peaked, so he gets in at the top. Then the market turns down and he sells in a panic to avoid taking the big loss. It has been my observation that the net transaction is a loss, with rare exception.

If you are one of those people who can dollar average your stock purchases, meaning that you continue to invest in the blue chips during good times and bad, you will do okay. But it also means that you have probably just moved out of the average or novice category, in which case you would be better off switching your investment over to mutual funds where a knowledgeable professional with a proven track record will manage your stocks for you.

You may or may not agree with my worst investment list, but I developed it by observing how others have consistently lost their hard-earned money over the years. Some people have beaten the system and walked away with their earnings. But on the average the people I counsel are not professional investors, and they range in incomes all the way from half a million dollars a year to less than $10,000. Some are college graduates; some have not completed high school. Some are senior citizens; others are just starting out. The point is, they represent the average American investor pretty well, both Christian and non-Christian. Most would heartily agree that had they avoided these "worst investments" they would have been much better off financially today. But that decision is up to you. As Proverbs 18:15 says: "The mind of the prudent acquires knowledge, and the ear of the wise seeks knowledge."

5

The Best Investments

Since I don't want to seem anti-investment orient- ed, I decided to include a chapter on the invest- ments that have worked out best for those I have coun- seled. This in no way implies that everyone who selected one of these investments made money with it, any more than those who selected the previous group always lost money. But on the average, more people made money using these investments than lost money.

BEST INVESTMENT #1:
A HOME

If you have your home paid off at age 60 or earlier, you have made what has been, without question, the best overall investment for the majority of Americans. Resi- dential housing has kept track with inflation and appreciated approximately 4 percent a year besides. That doesn't make it the best growth investment, but it does make it the best performer for the average individual.

It is also important to remember that our homes serve a purpose beyond the investment sphere. A home is something that you can use while it appreciates.

Many investment analysts have recently commented that the boom in residential housing is over. That is probably true to some extent. I believe that the expansion of single-family residences via cheap credit is winding down and housing will be more expensive for young couples. But Americans are hooked on having their own homes. If that trend changes it will only be because the country is in the midst of another Great Depression, in which case all other investments are equally at risk.

The most common argument against paying off a home mortgage early is the loss of the tax deduction for the interest. Allow me to expose this myth once and for all.

Let's assume that you are in a 30 percent federal tax bracket and a 6 percent state tax bracket. We'll also forget that the tax rates are graduated (based on a lower percentage at lower incomes). For each $1,000 in interest you pay on a home mortgage, you will receive 30 percent of it from the IRS and 6 percent from the state, right? ($1,000 x 30% = $300; $1,000 x 6% = $60.) So you will net $360 for your $1,000 interest payment. What happened to the other $640 you paid in interest?

As best I can tell, the mortgage company kept your money and you only received a portion of it back through tax deductions. What would happen if instead of paying interest on a mortgage you simply paid the taxes?

You would owe $360 in federal and state income taxes but would keep $640. I'm not an investment counselor, but that seems like a better deal to me.

BEST INVESTMENT #2:
RENTAL PROPERTIES

It has often been said that the thing you know best, you do best. The majority of Americans know how to evaluate rental properties, particularly residential housing. Most of us have been renters ourselves at one time or another, or have bought and sold homes. Most homeowners have the ability to evaluate good rental real estate — at least when compared to buying soybeans, stocks, or coins. Therefore, rental properties are a logical source of investments — but not for everyone.

There are assets and liabilities to owning rental properties. Unless you have a strong personality and are willing to eject some nonpaying tenants from time to time, you need to avoid becoming a landlord.

A friend who has done exceedingly well in residential rentals over the years has a philosophy that I endorse. First, he sets his rent levels at less than the going market rates in his area. This is so he will attract a good volume of potential renters and can then qualify them according to the criteria he has established over the years, which include credit checks, previous rentals, and personal references. His low-rent policy also helps to attract long-term tenants who know they could never duplicate the deal he has provided them.

He establishes his rental rates on the basis of covering his mortgage payments and other out-of-pocket costs, including that of maintaining the properties. His goal has always been to use the rental income to pay off the mortgages, and then use the mortgage payment money for his retirement income. During the first 10 to 15 years he receives very little, if any, personal income from the rentals. Yet he now owns several dozen rental houses debt-free and has a sizable, and very stable, income.

Often he has shared stories of renters who have maintained the properties at their own expense, including one who totally reroofed a home because he did not want his rent to go up. This is one of the rare win-win situations with rental properties.

One of the most attractive aspects of rental property is that the initial investment is not excessively large in many areas. An additional benefit is that once the property is rented the tenants pay off the mortgage for you.

Many investors have moved up from single-family rentals to duplexes or triplexes because the risk is reduced. The chances of a unit being vacant are cut proportionately to the number of tenants it will accommodate. The flipside of the coin is that the initial costs also go up, and often to buy such a unit requires a partnership arrangement with someone else.

If you have accumulated some cash reserves by now, you may want to consider entering a joint venture in a rental home with a couple who will live in it. Usually this means that you, as the investor, will provide the down payment and assume a 50-percent (negotiable) interest in the property. The tenant couple then will pay the mortgage payments and all other associated costs, including maintenance. When the house is resold, usually after no more than 10 years, the investor receives the down payment back and the two parties split the profits equally. There is a risk that the property will not appreciate, but that is the risk you run with any investment.

BEST INVESTMENT #3:
MUTUAL FUNDS

The whole concept of mutual funds is designed to attract the average investor. The pooling of a large number of small investors' moneys to buy a broad diversity of stocks (and other securities) is a simple way of spreading the risks.

Most of the average-income families I know who have accumulated supplemental income for education or retirement have done so successfully through the use of mutual funds. I particularly like mutual funds because (1) most allow small incremental investments, (2) they provide professional investment management, and (3) they allow great flexibility through the shifting of funds between a variety of investment assets.

As with any other area of investing, you must exercise caution and acquire some fundamental knowledge of what you're doing. There are funds that perform well in good economies and then lose it all in economic downturns. There are funds that guessed right once and basically never duplicated the feat again. There are funds that charge excessive administrative fees and dilute the return to their investors. And there are funds that have performed well for two and three decades and continue to lead the industry.

Even with these, you must exercise some caution, because their success may be built around the expertise of a single individual. When that person retires or dies, the fund may lose its edge. It is well worth an investment of $50 to $100 a year to subscribe to a good mutual fund newsletter if you have $10,000 or more to invest. It will help you to keep close tabs on the fund(s) you select.

Mutual funds offer such a diversity of investment products that it is probably safe to say that if you want to invest in anything legitimate there is a fund that will allow you to do so. Since we're going to evaluate some of the various fund types that are available in a later chapter, I will not elaborate here.

It is important to note, however, that in placing mutual funds in the best investments category I need to offer a qualifier. A good-quality, well-managed fund fits in that description. A poor-quality, poorly managed one does not. Later we will discuss how to find the funds that have proven to be the most reliable to the average investor.

Just remember that just as stocks are more speculative than corporate bonds, and bonds are more speculative than CDs, and CDs are more speculative than Treasury bills, mutual funds fit the same profile. So the type of fund you invest in will greatly affect the risk of your money, even in the well-managed ones. The higher the promised return, the greater the risk that must be assumed and, therefore, the less attractive it is to people age 60 and over.

A growth (speculative stock) mutual fund managed by the best advisor in the world is still more risky than a mutual fund that invests only in U.S. Treasury securities.

The question of whether to invest in a loaded or no-load fund always comes up in any discussion of mutual funds. A "loaded" mutual fund means that the sales commissions and administrative fees are taken out of the purchase price of the fund up front. For instance, a $5,000 investment in a fund with a 6 percent load would actually leave $4,700 to be invested in the fund. Additionally, you may also be charged an annual fee that can vary from a few dollars to several hundred or more, depending on the amount invested.

A "no-load" fund means that no commissions or fees are deducted up front. Logically an investor should therefore conclude that a no-load fund is better since 100 percent of your money goes into the investment. That may or may not be true in the long run. If the no-load fund has higher annual fees and commissions, the money you save up front can quickly be consumed in the first few years, and then some.

77

I personally have found that a well-managed no-load fund will beat a well-managed loaded fund; therefore, that is what I look for. But a well-managed loaded fund is a better buy than a poorly managed no-load. So choose your fund carefully. The primary reason a loaded fund is loaded is because of sales commissions. If you need individualized help in selecting or understanding mutual funds, the fees may be worth it to you. The no-load funds sell their products through advertising, not agents. They will provide any information you need by phone or mail, but use no local sales agents. It is my opinion that a subscription to a good mutual fund newsletter is better than paying a commission, but you may disagree if you know an honest, knowledgeable agent.

As with most investments today, one of the primary difficulties with mutual funds is trying to decide which type of fund best suits your individual need and which company's products are the best. With the hundreds of choices and every salesperson (by phone or in person) totally convinced that his or her products are the best, it can be very confusing.

BEST INVESTMENT #4:
INSURANCE PRODUCTS

I have found in teaching finances on a daily radio program that there is no better way to stir up a heated debate than to discuss insurance. It really doesn't matter what position I take: If I am for insurance or against it (or totally neutral), I'm always stepping on somebody's toes because so many people earn their salaries in the insurance industry.

If you would care to read a thorough discussion on insurance from a biblical perspective, as well as the assets and liabilities of term versus whole life, see my book, *The Complete Financial Guide for Young Couples* (Victor Books, 1989). But for the purposes of this particular book, I'll limit my evaluation to the investment side of insurance.

Over the past 20 years or so, insurance companies have developed many investment products to tap into the private retirement savings movement. Products like cash-value insurance and annuities have been around for nearly a hundred years, but they were not really competitive as investment vehicles until more recently, in my opinion.

Generally speaking, the accumulated savings in life insurance was, and still is, too accessible to the investor. Therefore, the majority of investors look upon their cash values as a ready source of funds in a time of need. That's fine if the intent is to build a reserve account for a new car, a down payment for a home, or even a college tuition fund. But there are many places to save money at higher rates of interest than a whole life insurance policy. Besides, stripping life insurance of its cash values reduces the amount of insurance available in the event of the insured's death.

During the decade of the eighties, as retirement plans such as IRAs, Keoghs, 401 (k)s, and the like became available to the general public, the insurance companies realized they had to pay higher rates of return if they were to be competitive as investment companies. The insurance companies also realized that the higher yielding mutual funds would eventually pull capital out of existing insurance policies. A knowledgeable investor would not leave money in a cash-value insurance policy at 4 to 6 percent return when mutual funds were earning twice that per year. Consequently, the major insurance companies began to offer policies with much higher yields. With the dual benefit of insurance coverage, plus higher yields, they became viable products for long-term investors.

The two basic types of insurance plans used most often (by those whom I have counseled) are annuities and whole-life insurance (usually in specialized policies such as universal life). There are endless varieties of these plans available. The difficulties are to determine which best suits your investment needs, and then to decide which company offers the highest return with the lowest risk. I have included a chapter on evaluating investments, which covers insurance products, so I will not elaborate on them here.

Generally speaking, insurance products have been among the safest, if not the highest earning, investments. But what has been safe in the past does not automatically imply future safety. The insurance industry as a whole is very sound, but several of the larger companies have made many bad investments. The future of some insurance companies is in jeopardy. It is critical to select the company you use carefully and continue to monitor it at least annually, just as you would any other investment.

It would be far better to withdraw your cash reserves from a policy, or transfer your savings in an annuity, even if there is a penalty to do so, than to risk losing it all.

BEST INVESTMENT #5:
COMPANY RETIREMENT PLANS

You may be past the age to consider this as an option, but I will include it for those who might still be able to take advantage of a company-sponsored retirement plan. The jargon used to identify these plans may be confusing, with titles like 401 (k), 403 (b), TSA, HR-10, and the like. But, in reality, the titles simply reference the tax codes that authorize the plans.

The investments available through a company retirement plan are the same as those you might choose personally. Depending on the plan and how it is administered, your options can include annuities, mutual funds, company stock, CDs, or any combination of these.

The disadvantage of a company retirement plan is that although you may be able to select any of several investment options, the plan administrator(s) selects the plan's options. They may or may not be the best options available to meet your personal goals.

One large advantage of company-sponsored retirement plans is that usually the funds invested are tax deferred (delayed until withdrawal). Additionally, many companies offer matching funds based on a percentage of what you elect to invest yourself. Some companies even go so far as to provide 100 percent of the retirement funds. I trust there is no one foolish enough to turn down an offer like that.

There are some potential problems with company retirement accounts. You need to be aware of these and take the proper precautions.

1. The plan administrator may invest poorly, thus placing your funds in risk.

2. The company may reserve the right to borrow from the employees' retirement account for operating capital. The problem here is that if the company fails, the retirement plan may fail too, especially if the company has substituted its own stock as collateral for the loans.

3. The company may reserve the right to borrow from the retirement account and substitute an insurance annuity for the cash. If the insurance company itself fails, then the retirement plan fails too.

Even with these potential problems, company-sponsored retirement plans represent one of the best investments for any average investor. Most companies are run honestly and ethically and have the best interests of their employees at heart. Just be aware of the potential problems and do the checking necessary to verify the solvency of your plan.

Remember, the sooner you start in a retirement plan, the less risk you will have to assume in order to reach your financial goals. Sometimes it is advantageous to invest in a company retirement plan even before paying off a home mortgage, especially if the company matches the funds at a rate of 25 percent or more. It's hard to beat an investment where someone guarantees you a 25 percent return the first year — tax free!

BEST INVESTMENT #6:
GOVERNMENT-BACKED SECURITIES

In pondering what to include in the best investments section I have tried not to get too detailed, lest we both get bogged down in whether a municipal bond from Chicago is better than one from New York. That kind of analysis is difficult at best since risk factors can change so quickly. So I purposely limited the discussion to general areas of investment. Government-backed investments are considered to be absolute security. Among those I have counseled who were older than 50 years of age, government-backed securities dominated their best investments list.

This does not imply that securities such as CDs, T-bills, bonds, and the like are the best performers. As mentioned earlier, they are usually selected for their lack of risk, not their return.

Once you have saved enough to meet your investment goals, the shift to government-backed securities is logical. Why leave your money at risk if you don't need to? Obviously your plans need to compensate for inflation, but the ratios should swing decidedly toward the safe side as you get older. Simply put, it is more difficult, if not impossible, for most older people to replace their investment funds; so the older you are, the more conservative you should become in your investing.

6

The Five-Tier System

I would like to present briefly some of the more common investments available and place them on what I refer to as the "tiered" system (tiered according to how I rate them for risk and return). I trust this will help you later as you consider which investments are right for your plan. (NOTE: This is an expansion of material I have previously covered in my book *The Complete Financial Guide for Young Couples.*)

I have simply assigned a scale from 0 to 10 that can be applied to each type of investment. Zero represents the least return or the least risk, and 10 represents the highest risk or highest return. Therefore, an investment with an income potential of 0 and a risk factor of 10 would represent the worst possible investment. An investment with an income potential of 10 and a risk of 0 would be the best investment. You can't find those, by the way.

I have also added a third factor: growth. Growth means the ability of an investment to appreciate, such as common stocks. Investments such as bonds have a potential growth factor also. If a bond pays a yield of 10 percent and interest rates drop to 8 percent, the bond value increases, and vice versa.

The investments will be divided into the five basic tiers:

Tier 1. *Secure Income:* Selected because it generates cash with very little risk.

Tier 2. *Long-Term:* Selected for stability of earnings for one-year deposits or longer.

Tier 3. *Growth Investments:* Selected primarily for long-term appreciation.

Tier 4. *Speculative:* A mix between growth and speculation.

Tier 5. *High-Risk:* Selected for their volatility and maximum growth potential.

Remember that the rating for each type of investment is purely my evaluation. It should not be accepted as an absolute. Times and economic conditions constantly change, and the degree of return or risk for most types of investments will change with the economy. When interest rates and inflation are high, real property, residential housing, apartment complexes, or office buildings generally do well. But when interest rates and inflation are down, stocks and bonds generally do well.

TIER 1: SECURE INCOME INVESTMENTS

Government Securities — Income 5; Growth 0; Risk 1
Treasury bills (T-bills), Government National Mortgage Association bonds (Ginnie Maes), and savings bonds fall into this category.

Bank Securities — Income 5; Growth 0; Risk 3-4
One advantage of bank investments, such as savings accounts, CDs, and insured money funds, is that you can invest with smaller amounts of money. The disadvantages are that they offer little or no growth because the payout is fixed; and the income is taxable as it is earned.

TIER 2: LONG-TERM INCOME INVESTMENTS

Municipal Bonds — Income 5; Growth 0; Risk 7-8
These are bonds issued by a local municipality, usually a larger city. Most or all of the income from such bonds is exempt from federal income tax (and state income tax in the state where they are issued).

The liabilities of municipal bonds are (1) they have low yields; (2) they normally require a large initial investment; and (3) they are illiquid, meaning that if you have to sell them, you will normally do so at a loss.

Mortgages — Income 8; Growth 0; Risk 3-4
A mortgage is a contract to lend someone money to buy a home or other real property. Mortgage repurchase agreements are commonly offered by commercial

lenders who want to resell loans they have made. The seller normally discounts the mortgage to yield from 1 to 3 percent above prevailing interest rates.

The risk on this type of investment is relatively low because you have real property backing the loan. If a borrower fails to pay, you can foreclose on the property. The liabilities are: (1) they are hard to find; (2) the return on your investment is 100 percent taxable; (3) there is no growth on your principal, unless interest rates drop; and (4) your money will usually be tied up for a period of 15 to 20 years.

Second mortgages usually yield a higher return, but there is an equivalent higher risk, including the fact that in case the borrower defaults it is more difficult to foreclose.

Corporate Bonds — Income 6-8; Growth 0-3; Risk 5-6
A corporate bond is a note issued by a corporation to finance its operation. Quality bonds often yield 2 to 3 percent higher interest rates than an equivalent CD or T-bill. Bonds are rated from a low of C to a high of AAA. The higher the rating the lower the rate of return, but the risk is lower as well. One liability of corporate bonds is that repayment depends on the success of *one* company. Also, the income is totally taxable.

Insurance Annuities — Income 3-4; Growth 0; Risk 5-6
This investment requires a prescribed amount of money to be paid into the annuity, and then the issuing insurance company promises a monthly income after

retirement age. The advantages of annuities are that the earnings accumulate, tax deferred, until you retire; you can usually get your money out if you need to (although there is often a penalty); and, compared to other tax-sheltered investments, the returns are good.

But be aware that the stated yield of an insurance annuity isn't necessarily what you will receive. Ask for a net figure that doesn't include administrative and other costs; and get all quotes in writing.

Stock Dividends — Income 4-5; Growth 0-10; Risk 6-7
Common stocks usually pay dividends based on the earnings of the company. One advantage is that stocks can be purchased for relatively small amounts of money. It's possible to invest in a stock paying a dividend of 7 to 8 percent and invest less than $100. This obviously appeals to the small investor. Since the dividend is totally related to the success of the issuing company, I would look for a company that has paid dividends for many years, particularly during economic hard times. Be aware, though, that just because a corporation has paid dividends for decades doesn't necessarily mean that it can continue to do so.

As stated previously, a good quality mutual fund can lessen the risk while achieving the same results. Professional management, together with broad diversification, provide a great advantage.

Money Funds — Income 4-5; Growth 0; Risk 2-8
Money funds are the pooled funds of many people used to purchase short-term securities. These are not

true savings accounts, but are short-term mutual funds that pay interest. Shares normally sell for $1 each but can vary, depending on the fund's assets value. Money funds are available through most brokerage firms, savings and loans, and banks; those offered by brokerage firms are not federally insured against losses. The interest rates are normally adjusted monthly.

It is extremely important to verify the rating of any money fund frequently. If the rating drops below an "A," remove your money and select another fund. Also, don't maintain more than $25,000 or 10 percent of your assets (whichever is lower) in any one money fund.

TIER 3: GROWTH INVESTMENTS

This tier is in the middle and represents the crossover from conservative to speculative investments. During one cycle of the economy these investments may appear to be conservative, but then during the next cycle they appear to be speculative.

Undeveloped Land — Income 0-2; Growth 6-7; Risk 3-4

During the highly inflationary seventies, farmland and other undeveloped properties were good investments. People speculated in land just as they did in income properties. This drove prices up and, unfortunately, tempted even farmers to speculate.

The eighties saw inflation subside and land prices level out. Consequently, raw land prices also fell. Today an investment in raw land is considered fairly conservative, although there is a risk if the purchase is leveraged. The prospect of the kind of growth seen in the seventies and eighties is considered unlikely, but this scenario can and will change again as the economy changes.

Housing—Income 5-7; Growth 0-5; Risk 3-4

As noted previously, no investment during the last 25 years has been consistently better for the average investor than single-family rental houses. That doesn't mean that residential properties will appreciate the way they did over the last two decades, but I can see no long-range trends away from rental housing in the next decade. In fact, with the Tax Reform Act making multi-family housing less attractive to investors, fewer apartments will probably be built during the nineties. That should place more value on rental housing.

One advantage of investing in rental housing is that it can be done with a relatively small initial down payment. When investing in rental properties, the most important principle to remember is: no surety. If the house won't stand as collateral for its own mortgage, pass it by.

Rental housing not only generates income but also shelters much of that income through depreciation, interest, and taxes. The 1986 Tax Reform Act placed limits on what can be deducted for tax purposes against ordinary income, and it's entirely possible that future tax changes will affect real property even more. But I still believe rental housing promises good growth through the end of this century, barring an economic catastrophe.

Negatives to consider before investing in rental housing are: (1) if you don't want to be a landlord, don't buy rental housing; (2) if you aren't able to maintain and manage your own property, many of the benefits decline; (3) it's not always easy to get your money out if you need it.

Remember the three key factors about buying any rental property, whether it is a single-family house, duplex, or triplex: location, location, location.

Mutual Funds — Income 6-8; Growth 4-5; Risk 4-5

A mutual fund is an investment pool for many small investors. A group of professional advisors invests for them, usually in the stock or bond markets. There are specialized mutual funds that invest in automobiles, precious metals, utility companies, government securities, and so forth. In fact, you can find a mutual fund for almost any area in which you want to invest.

Mutual funds are valuable for the small investor for several reasons. (1) You can invest with a relatively small amount of money (many mutual funds require as little as $500). (2) Your money is spread over a large area in the economy. (3) The return on the best mutual funds has averaged more than twice the prevailing interest rates for any 10-year period.

I would encourage any potential investor in mutual funds to go to independent sources and check out the fund first. Since we are discussing growth mutual funds, it is important to verify the track record and projected earnings of any fund you might select. A prospectus from the mutual fund company will clearly define the "secure" or low-risk funds and the "growth" or speculative funds.

I prefer to use no-load (non-commission) funds, because they allow my money to grow without the service fees or commissions coming out of the initial investment. But even no-load funds will normally carry some penalties if you decide to withdraw your money during the first five years.

TIER 4: SPECULATIVE INVESTMENTS

Common Stocks/Mutual Funds —
Income 2-8; Growth 0-7; Risk 7-8

Again, the advantages of common stocks are that you can invest with a relatively small amount of money and potential exists for sizable growth. The liabilities of common stocks are obvious. First, you can suffer a loss as easily as you can make a profit. Second, stocks require buying and selling to maximize their potential and consequently require broker fees. If you expect to make money in common stocks, you're probably going to have to trade them periodically. If you're not willing to do that, it's better to stick with other kinds of investments.

Precious Metals — Income 0; Growth 0-8; Risk 8-9

As mentioned before, precious metals such as gold, silver, or platinum can be purchased either for long-term growth or pure speculation. For long-term growth, buy the metal, put it in a safety deposit box, and hope it appreciates over a period of time. Most people do this primarily as a hedge against a potential calamity in the economy. In an economy as unstable as ours, a small percentage of your assets invested in precious metals can help to balance other assets more vulnerable to inflation. When buying and selling anything, especially precious metals, it's wise to remember what Baruch said: "Buy when they sell. Sell when they buy." Keep a long-term mentality about precious metals — at least those you invest in as a hedge.

TIER 5: HIGH-RISK INVESTMENTS

These investments should play only a relatively small part (5 to 10 percent at the most) in any investment plan. Their primary value is the potential appreciation — speculation. Most generate little or no income and are highly volatile.

Gold/Silver — Income 0; Growth 0-10; Risk 9-10

You can invest in precious metals both for long-term growth and for short-term speculation. This would be most beneficial in a highly volatile economy where major changes were occurring, such as the oil crisis in the mid-seventies or the run-up in silver prices in the late seventies. Obviously, such events are difficult to predict and are extremely risky. They are for the investor with a strong heart and cash only. Unless you are a professional investor, this is probably not an area where you want to risk a lot of money.

Oil and Gas — Income 0-8; Growth 0-10; Risk 10+
In the late seventies and early eighties when crude oil prices cycled up, oil and gas investments were the hottest things going. But many people who invested money in oil and gas did not understand the risks involved, and the vast majority lost their investments when the prices fell and marginal wells became unprofitable. A high degree of risk exists, particularly in oil exploration. If you plan to invest in oil and gas, risk only a small portion of your assets.

Commodities Market —
Income 0; Growth 0-10; Risk 10+
Commodities speculation requires a relatively small dollar investment and can bring huge returns, primarily through the use of leverage. An example of leverage is using a $1,000 investment in the commodities market to control $10,000 worth of contracts — or more — for future delivery. If that sounds good, remember this: "A fool and his money are soon parted." Approximately 1 out of every 200 people who invest in the commodities market ever gets any money back. It is pure gambling. You can lose everything you own, and even more.

Collectibles — Income 0; Growth 2-10; Risk 10+
Antiques, old automobiles, paintings, and figurines are all collectibles that can be used while you hold them to sell. To invest in these successfully you need to know their value, the best places to buy and sell, and you

need to have the capital and the patience to wait for just the right buyer.

Precious Gems — Income 0; Growth 0-4; Risk 10+
Diamonds, opals, rubies, sapphires, and other stones can be purchased for relatively small amounts of money. For every person I know who made money in gems, I know a hundred who lost money. It's almost impossible for a novice to know the true value of a gem, even with a "certified" appraisal. Worst of all, it's very difficult to sell gems at a fair price unless you have your own market. The rule here is to stay with what you know or with someone you thoroughly trust.

Limited Partnerships —
Income 0-7; Growth 0; Risk 10+
Limited partnerships are formed to pool investors' money to purchase assets, usually in real properties. Since your investment in a limited partnership is no better than the property and the management, the key is to know the general partner and his credibility. Limit your liability to only the money you have at risk. For most investors, the risk is too high and the returns too uncertain.

HOW THE TIERS CAN WORK

As an example of how the tier approach can work, let's suppose a widow, age 68, has $130,000 in cash to invest. Her goals are to supplement her Social Security income by $500 a month, and leave her estate to her children upon her death.

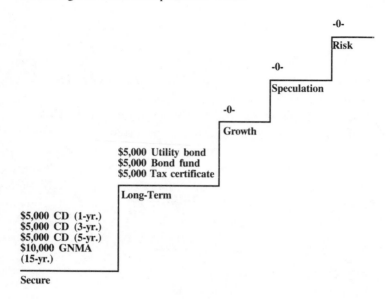

Total Return = $10,000/year

As you can see, her strategy is weighed heavily toward the low-risk tiers because she can meet all of her goals without assuming any significant risk. Her investments also provide her with adequate liquidity in the event she needs cash for medical expenses or other emergencies. In the event that inflation picks up and begins to erode her assets, most of them are renewable in five years or less so she can reinvest at higher interest rates when necessary.

Consider another case: An employee of a car manufacturer, with $30,000 to invest at age 62. His goals are to retire this year on Social Security and company retirement income of approximately $2,000 per month combined, and to use his surplus savings for travel and additional spending that his retirement income will not allow.

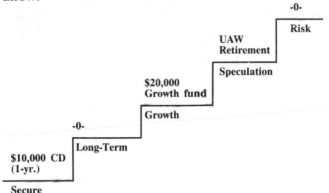

I have mapped this man's retirement account as a part of his investment program because it is, even though he has virtually no control over it. The $30,000 savings is divided into emergency savings and growth income. His risk is slightly higher than would be normal for a 62-year-old with limited assets, but since he does not require the funds to live on, he can maximize the return without too much risk. His average annual yield should be 10 to 12 percent.

You don't necessarily need to lay out your financial goals in a tier plan. I do this because it makes the examples simpler. The principle is the same whether you diagram or write out your goals: *You need to make very specific plans if you ever hope to accomplish them.*

Both spouses need to discuss their long-range goals and commit them to prayer. Until you do, why should you believe that God will entrust more to you? As Jesus said in Luke 16:10, "He who is faithful in a very little thing is faithful also in much; and he who is unrighteous in a very little thing is unrighteous also in much." Manage well the portion that you now have and God will be able to entrust even more to you.

7

Evaluating Investments

Now let's get down to specifics. Let's say that you've arrived at age 60-plus with your living expenses under the control of a budget and some funds to invest. Remember that at this stage of life you will usually be looking for low-risk investments. It may help to consider this overall view of the options before you.

On the surface, deciding where to put your cash would not seem very complicated. But the competition among banks and other financial institutions in recent years has given rise to a bewildering number of options.

BANK SAVINGS

The majority of American investors still keep their cash reserves in banks. Total cash reserves in banks as of 1991 were nearly twice that of all other consumer accounts at brokerage firms, credit unions, etc. Cash deposit accounts at banks can be broken down into three basic categories.

Passbook Accounts

These are unrestricted accounts that usually pay the minimum amount of interest, while allowing the depositor daily access to the funds. Usually a transaction fee is levied if the account is used more than a few times each month. The only advantage I can see with these accounts is that they will allow deposits as little as $10. Once the minimum amount necessary to qualify for a money market account is reached, the funds should be transferred.

Money Market Accounts

These can go under a variety of titles such as "Golden Passbook," "Ready Cash Account," "Preferred Investors Account," and so on. These accounts were established to compete directly with the brokerage firms' accounts that were attracting much of the small depositors' cash in the early eighties. Some may have limited checking, but most also offer a variety of free services.

Certificates of Deposit

These are time deposit accounts that can vary from three months to several years. Usually the longer the time and the larger the deposit, the higher the interest rate the account earns. Usually there is a penalty for early withdrawal.

A liability of all three of these cash accounts is that

any income is taxable as it is earned, unless it is held in a qualified retirement account.

BROKERAGE FIRM ACCOUNTS

Most brokerage firms offer a variety of cash investments, including the resale of most local, state, and federal government loans. Perhaps the most common type of brokerage firm account is the money market fund. These are mutual funds that allow you to withdraw your cash as needed. Many also provide check-writing privileges. The interest earned by these funds usually reflects the risk they take with your investment dollars.

CREDIT UNIONS

The growth of credit unions in the U.S. has been significant over the last two decades. They usually offer 1 to 2 percent higher interest rates than the banks. Credit unions are now insured by the FDIC, and in my opinion they are probably as safe or safer than banks. If you invest with a credit union, be sure it is a member of the National Association of Credit Unions and is fiscally sound.

INSURANCE COMPANIES

In the past, the interest paid on cash values in life insurance plans was meager but dependable. Because of intense competition, insurance companies have been forced to increase their rate of returns, and this has meant taking on greater risks. As I said earlier, I believe you should look at insurance as provision in the case of premature death, not as an investment.

BONDS AND BOND FUNDS

Bonds

Bonds are the primary obligation of the issuer. The issuer can be an individual, a business, or a local, state, or federal government. Most brokerage firms sell bonds (and bond funds) for a small fee. The interest promised on any bond is directly related to three basic factors: the length of deposit, the amount invested, and the rating of the bond issuer.

It is arguable that some corporate bonds are probably safer than many government bonds. A major corporation like IBM may well be more solvent than a municipality like New York or Philadelphia. Actually a company, such as IBM, is probably sounder than the federal government, although the federal government does have the unique ability to print money.

Usually an investment in a specific bond is for a predetermined period of time. Thus the principal invested is not readily available unless the bond is resold. The face value of a bond can fluctuate according to the prevailing interest rates. For instance, if you purchase a bond for $1,000 paying 10 percent interest and the market rate drops to 8 percent, your bond will probably go up in value. If the prevailing market rate climbs to 12 percent, the bond value will probably drop. The actual increase or decrease in value is what makes the bond market volatile. As discussed previously, it is also what tempts the commodities dealers to gamble on the future value of bonds.

Bond Funds

Bond funds represent the best option for the majority of average investors, in my opinion. The diversification they offer helps to lessen the fluctuations in value and risk. Most bond funds also offer the option of buying and selling the shares without the penalty an ordinary bond would carry. It is important to select the bond funds with the same degree of caution that you would a specific bond. The security and dependability of the fund is directly related to where the fund invests its assets. For maximum safety, select the all-government fund. For higher income, select the corporate fund. For maximum income (and risk), funds made up of repurchased junk bonds, Third World debt, and the like, are available.

Bonds are rated according to a complex formula that takes into account the company's (or government's) projected ability to repay under the most adverse of circumstances. These ratings from the rating services change regularly if the risk of the bond issuer changes. The best bonds, and bond funds, carry a AAA rating. The riskiest carry a C rating or less. For the average investor, any bond or bond fund with a rating of less than AA should be considered risky. Most of the financial analysts I spoke with about rating services tended to depend more on the Standard and Poor's service because of the way they gathered the data on the bond issuers. For an interested investor, this information is available by subscribing to one of the bond-related newsletters.

Zero Coupon Bonds

A zero coupon bond is actually a note issued by a company or government agency at a discount. For example, a 10-year bond with a redemption value of $1,000 may be sold to an investor for $700. No interest or dividends are paid during the term (hence the name "zero coupon"). A more traditional bond has interest-bearing coupons that can be clipped and redeemed during the holding period.

Government Bonds

There are three basic types of cash investments marketed directly by the federal government: savings bonds, Treasury bills (T-bills), and Treasury bonds.

Savings bonds. These bonds are loans to the government for a predetermined period of time (usually seven years or longer). They are considered to be very secure, and the interest earned is not taxed until the bond is redeemed at maturity.

Treasury bills. T-bills are also loans made to the government. The interest they pay is usually about 1 percent less than the current rates earned by CDs.

Treasury bonds and notes. These are usually offered in larger denominations of $25,000 or more, and for periods of up to 30 years. They constitute the government's basic method of financing its long-term debt. The interest rates vary with the prevailing markets, but usually are at least 1 percent lower than equivalent bank CDs and several percentage points lower than the equivalent corporate bonds.

Ginnie Maes

We have noted that these are bonds issued by the Government National Mortgage Association, and they are actually a composite of mortgage loans guaranteed by the federal government and resold to the public. Ginnie Maes can be purchased in units of $10,000 or more.

The single largest negative of bonds like Ginnie Maes is that the borrowers have the option to prepay their loans at any time. So although you may purchase a Ginnie Mae bond expecting to receive your prescribed interest for the term of the bond, if the interest rates drop and the borrower elects to refinance and thus pays off your bond, you have no option. You may well find yourself trying to reinvest your funds at substantially lower interest rates.

TAX CERTIFICATES

A little-known and seldom-utilized type of bond is a municipal tax certificate. This is a lien that a municipality places on a taxpayer's property for delinquent taxes.

The buyer (lender) of a tax certificate is legally the lienholder on the property. If the certificate is not repaid with the accumulated interest before the statute of limitations for tax liens expires (three years in most states), the lender can foreclose on the property, thereby assuming all the rights of the property owner.

The interest rate assigned to tax certificates is usually significantly higher than the prime interest rate.

Keep in mind the rule of risk and return. The reason the rate is higher is the inherent risk involved. When you purchase a tax certificate you can acquire no greater rights than the taxpayer. If there is an outstanding mortgage, you must assume that loan. If the property has a title flaw, you will assume that too. It is important to investigate carefully the collateral backing the certificate you purchase. Information on tax certificates can be obtained from most county tax offices.

CHURCH BONDS

I have included this category of bonds because of their prevalence in the Christian community. These are loans made to a church (normally) to fund a building program. Two significant points need to be made here:

1. *It is my conclusion, based on my study of God's Word, that loans to Christians (and Christian organizations such as a church) should be made without interest.* If you would like to study this topic for yourself, I would direct you to the following Scriptures: Leviticus 25:35-37, Deuteronomy 23:19-20, Nehemiah 5:7-10, and Psalm 15:5. (There are several other references about lending without interest to God's people, but these will give you an overview.) Then you must decide for yourself whether or not you believe this principle is applicable to God's people today; personally, I do.

2. *Church bonds are high-risk loans and should be made only out of surplus funds that you can afford to lose if necessary.* I have counseled many Christians, including retirees and widows, who loaned money to a church

bond program that they should not have risked. Several lost their entire savings believing they were helping God's work and He would protect them. As best I can tell from God's Word, He is not in the lending business. When you lend, you're on your own.

JUNK BONDS

Junk bonds is a term used to describe many of the bonds that were used to finance leveraged buyouts of companies during the eighties. They are usually collateralized only by the good will of the issuer, and carry much higher than average interest rates.

Since the demise of the junk bond market in the early nineties, few new junk bonds have been issued or offered. However, many previously issued junk bonds are still floating around and are regularly resold to gullible investors. There are even junk bond funds established for the sole purpose of investing in these highly risky ventures. The high returns blind many investors who are foolish enough to think they can "beat the system."

UTILITY BONDS

The public utility companies throughout the country often finance new construction projects through long-term bonds. Over the last two decades, utility bonds (and stocks) have become the backbone of many investment plans. The advantages they offer are stability and relatively high interest rates.

However, utility bonds are not without risk themselves. Many investors who risked their money with utility companies in the seventies and eighties to build nuclear power-er facilities got a rude surprise as established utility companies defaulted on payments. Cost overruns and government regulations simply made many of these projects unprofitable. Although utility companies operate under a public utility license, they still must make a profit to repay creditors. Those that don't, can't.

Except for the bonds associated with nuclear power development, utility bonds have been rated among the best investments in America for nearly 70 years. For the average investor, the purchase of a utility bond fund probably makes more sense because the risk can be spread over many utility companies. The evidence of this logic can be seen in the fact that even when individual utility companies were defaulting on bonds attached to nuclear power facilities, the utility bond funds were still paying their investors. It is the simple principle of diversification.

MUNICIPAL BONDS

Local municipalities can issue interest-bearing bonds that are exempt from federal income taxes. Many states exempt the interest on bonds issued by municipalities within the state from state income taxes as well.

Because of this tax-exempt feature, municipal bonds are popular with higher income investors. However, it is easy to be beguiled by the promise of tax-free income. If you decide to invest in municipal bonds, or bond funds, you need to verify the rating of the issuing municipality. Several large cities are on the verge of insolvency and are able to pay the interest on existing bonds only by selling more bonds. This is very similar to a pyramid scheme in which only the early participants can get their money back. We have yet to see a major municipality default in our present generation. But I assure you, municipal bond holders during the Depression saw many municipalities default.

Also bear in mind that if your total tax rate is 40 percent, a totally taxable bond yielding 10 percent is the same as a tax-exempt bond yielding 6 percent. It may well be that the 10-percent bond is a better buy when risk is factored in.

STOCKS AND STOCK FUNDS

I have already warned that trading in stocks (and, to a lesser degree, in stock funds) is highly speculative. Stocks should be used only as growth investments for the preretirement years, or for surplus funds after retirement.

DISCOUNT BROKERS

As stated previously, discount brokerage firms place orders; they do not provide investment advice. When using a discount broker you must know what stocks, bonds, or other investments you want to buy. The broker simply places your order and charges a small fee for the service. Usually the fee is a small percentage of what a standard broker charges.

Probably the most widely known discount firm is Charles Schwab and Associates. This company started the current trend toward a nationwide use of discount brokerage firms in the early seventies. For stock or bond investors who need placement services only, a discount broker, like Schwab, can significantly reduce their trading costs.

The argument for using a discount broker is purely economic. More of your investment dollar goes into the investment. The argument against using a discount broker is that you receive no counsel when investing. In general, the decision to use or not to use discount services should be based on your ability to make investment decisions. If you don't need advice, why pay for it? If you do, the fee should be worth what you pay. The bottom line is, a fee-based broker should make you more than his fees cost you.

BLUE CHIP STOCKS

The so-called "Fortune 500" companies are often referred to as the blue chips (an obvious association with the higher value chips used on the tables in Las Vegas). These are some of the largest companies listed on the stock exchange, and represent the base value of American industry.

If an investor had simply spread his stock investments over the blue chip companies (or the Dow Jones list of companies used to establish the daily index) for the last 10 years, he would have earned approximately 10 percent annually in growth and dividends. There would have been some bad moments when it looked like the market would collapse as it did in the thirties, and nothing says it won't in the future, but overall, stocks were a better than average investment. It is the risk that makes them so volatile for the average investor, and the fact that outside of a balanced mutual fund it is difficult for most people to invest in a wide enough base of companies to lower the risk.

Normally good quality stocks are divided into two broad categories by investment analysts: *growth* and *income.*

Growth stocks are usually associated with newer companies, or emerging technologies. IBM was considered a growth stock in the early fifties. Xerox was a growth company in the sixties. Texas Instruments was a growth company in the seventies. Apple Computers became a growth company in the eighties. In the nineties the growth industry will probably be health-related companies. In the next century environmental companies could very well lead the way.

This does not mean that once a company has been a "growth company" that the stock does not appreciate. IBM is a good example of a company that has seen a steady growth pattern for more than three decades. But compared to the company's early days it would now be considered a stable income company.

Income stocks are selected primarily because of their stable, long-term income through dividends. Good examples of this type of investment would be utility stocks, automobile stocks, defense industry stocks, and the like. Once a company has established a decade-long track record of paying regular dividends, many investors seek them as a means to earn both income (through dividends) and growth (through stock appreciation). Often a company that is noted for its dividend payout will see its stock prices fall rapidly if the dividend is less than projected. On the other hand, a company selected primarily for growth may see its stock appreciate even though the company never declares a dividend.

It is important that you know which category a company's stock fits into when making an investment.

OVER-THE-COUNTER STOCKS

The cost of preparing a company's stock for sale on the national exchanges is prohibitively expensive for many emerging firms. In order for them to have a market for their stocks, the exchanges created the over-the-counter market. Stocks offered on this market are subject to less stringent Securities and Exchange rules as far as capitalization, income, and size are concerned. Basically these are speculative offerings of companies in the growth category. Buyers are presumed to be warned by the very fact that a stock is offered through the over-the-counter market.

Contained within this group of stocks are those often referred to as "penny" stocks. These probably represent the ultimate in risk of any stock regularly traded to the public.

The term *penny stock* refers to the very low price of the stocks, although not necessarily only pennies. When sales in these stocks began, the prices were actually a few pennies; since then the name has stuck. Investors in penny stocks should be advised that the risk is extremely high. These companies come and go regularly, rarely leaving any equity behind. The few that survive can appreciate greatly in value. But very few companies now traded on either exchange started as penny stock companies.

MUTUAL FUNDS

We have discussed how mutual funds pool investors' money to purchase a cross section of stocks or bonds. In order to attract investors in a very competitive field, mutual funds now offer a variety of options. One fund may range from growth stocks and blue chips to utilities, government bonds, and municipal bonds. Most funds now allow investors to shift their funds within a "family" of investments once or twice a year without penalty. This offers maximum diversification even for small investors.

When evaluating and projecting the future performance of a mutual fund, never rely on a one-year performance record. It may well be that the managers guessed right in a given market, but cannot duplicate the feat. A trained analyst can review a fund's performance and compare it with current management philosophy, cash position, and market position to come up with a reasonable projection of what the fund can do in the future.

REAL ESTATE

Without question, residential housing has been one of the most profitable areas of investment for most Americans for the last 40 or 50 years. The advent of the consumer credit boom that began after World War II provided the impetus for real estate appreciation, especially residential real estate. Simply put, more families were able to afford better housing through long-term financing.

The difficulty with any debt-financed expansion is that as the debt bubble expands it gets increasingly difficult to keep it inflated. The people who get in at the beginning make real profits since they can resell their expensive homes, move to a less expensive area of the country, and live on the surplus. But as the expansion continues there are fewer less expensive areas to move to and less appreciation in the existing homes. In a worst-case scenario the price of property drops as new buyers cannot manage the increasing monthly payments.

Once investors progress from residential real estate to other forms of real estate, such as commercial, farm land, and multi-family, the picture gets a lot cloudier. Some investors have done exceedingly well in high-growth areas like Florida and California. Others have done quite poorly in areas where the values rise and fall quickly. The oil patch in Texas and Oklahoma is a classic example of this fluctuating market. In these states, investing in real estate is much like investing in stocks; if you hit the right market you can make a lot of money. But if you hit the wrong market you can lose it all — and then some.

What I would like to do is discuss briefly each area of real estate investing and share some insights from others who have done well.

Residential Real Estate

The general rule for investing in rental housing is that 11 months of rental income must be able to cover 100 percent of all expenses, including payments, taxes, maintenance, and insurance. This leaves one month per year for income, or vacancy. The long-range strategy should be to have the property pay off the mortgage before you retire, so that the income is available then. A second alternative is to sell the property using owner financing. The mortgage payments then become a steady, dependable source of income after retirement.

A drawback here is that virtually no commercial lenders will finance real estate without a personal guarantee (surety). I have already warned of this; and unless I could find an owner-financed home or borrow, using only the property as collateral, I would not invest in rental housing.

Commercial Real Estate

For the vast majority of average investors, commercial real estate is beyond their financial resources, unless they pool their funds with other investors. I have already discussed the use of limited partnerships to do this in chapter 6, so I won't rehash that again. It is sufficient to say that unless you have a large degree of control over a project, you're generally better off pooling your investment money in a mutual fund where professional management is used.

From this point on, I will assume that those who will invest in commercial real estate have the financial ability to do so, and are not numbered among the faint-hearted. If these two elements are present (money and courage), a great deal of money can be made in commercial real estate. A review of those who attempted to get rich quick in commercial real estate should be sobering enough to frighten most investors out of the commercial real estate market. I will not attempt to discuss the details of investing in one of Donald Trump's hotels, or investing in multi-story office buildings. If that is your investment strategy, you probably won't be helped by reading this book. I suggest a good book on psychiatry instead!

In reality there are only a few investments in commercial real estate available to average investors. I will briefly discuss some of the more common opportunities.

Storage buildings. Some of the most profitable investments in commercial properties over the last 20 years have been mini-warehouse storage buildings. These are the small rental buildings used by many people for temporary storage space. The initial investment in these facilities is not insignificant. Often the cost of land, construction, and start-up advertising can run several thousand dollars per unit. But in good locations the storage units will repay all costs in five years or less. The obvious key is selecting the right location and analyzing the market carefully, including the competition.

Time-share condominiums. When the idea was first introduced in the late seventies and eighties, it caught on fast. Why should vacationers tie up a lot of money in a cramped motel room when, for a small investment, they could own a share in a condo and rent it out when they didn't want to use it?

Difficulties surfaced as more and more units were constructed and the competition for renters grew so fierce that finding them required large advertising budgets and steep discounts. Since the rental agencies were not going to take the losses, the only logical prospects were the absentee owners. Many investors found themselves stuck with a condo they couldn't use, high annual mortgage payments, maintenance fees, and rental costs, not to mention declining income from their units. Unless you really know what you're doing and can manage your own units in an area where you live, my counsel is to avoid them.

Lease-Repurchase Agreements

A popular concept that was developed in the eighties is selling rented office space to investors. I have several counselees who have invested in these situations and have done quite well. The concept is simple. A developer builds an office building and rents it out to qualified tenants. The rented offices are then resold to individual investors who become the owner/landlords. Assuming the tenants are stable and dependable businesses, the arrangement works well for all parties. Often the tenant will sign a lease agreement with an option to buy at a later date. A good office building can yield an average return of 20 percent a year, or more.

LAND SPECULATION

Virtually everyone in America knows of someone who struck it rich in the land business. Those who don't know someone certainly know someone who said they would have been rich had they just had the sense to invest in land 20 years ago. Tucked in the back of our minds somewhere is this secret desire to be one of those people who owned 10 acres in Kissimmee, Florida before Disney World came to town. I had a friend who owned 30 acres there and profited greatly. But it was purely by chance, not by design. But if you are bound and determined to invest, I would offer these suggestions:

1. *Buy only if you can see a future use for the property that will make it appreciate.* (For example, it's generally safe to buy raw land in a developing community where the property might eventually be going commercial or residential.)

2. *Plan to keep the property until it is totally paid off.* Don't anticipate selling it before a balloon payment comes due. If you can't handle the payments until it's paid off, don't take the risk.

3. *Buy only if the property can be used as total collateral for the loan (no surety).*

4. *Avoid joint ventures or partnerships to buy land.* Often what happens is the other parties can't pay their share and you will either have to pay for all of it or forfeit your equity.

COLLECTIBLES AND PRECIOUS METALS

Investing in collectibles such as coins, stamps, cards, and antiques is clearly more an art than a science. Yet collectible investing is truly a worldwide market today. Any auction of significance will draw bidders from every part of the globe.

The real key to making money through collectibles is expertise. You must know what you're doing or someone who does will sell you the proverbial "pig in a poke." Before you decide to risk any money on collectibles, I would encourage you to focus on one area (cards, stamps, porcelain), read all you can about it, attend a few auctions or shows, practice with "pretend" funds, and then start small.

Collectibles with Established Markets

Collectibles such as stamps, coins, sports cards, paintings, and antique furniture all have established markets or outlets. Some are traded through auctions. Others are traded through trade shows. Still others are traded through magazines. Some are bought and sold through all of the above. The advantage of having an established outlet is obvious. You may invest in a fine crystal glassware set that has good potential, but unless you can find a willing and able buyer you may not be able to resell it.

If you will invest a few dollars for some of the excellent books available on how to understand a particular collectible, you can avoid many hard lessons. Nothing can replace an instinct for finding the good deals. But there are two things to remember: *first,* the more you know, the easier making money becomes; *second,* in any investment field there are people with whom you will be competing.

Non-market Collectibles
Semi-precious stones have no readily available market, except from the dealer to the consumer. In such cases you must know how to create your own market — say by advertising or selling to friends and family. My counsel is to avoid this type of collectible unless you truly know what you're doing and can market them yourself.

Narrow Market Collectibles
This type includes investment-quality diamonds, works of art, historical documents, and the like. I term them narrow markets because an organized outlet usually exists, but access to it is limited to a few select dealers and brokers. So the average investor is excluded from access to the collectors except by random chance advertising.

Precious Metals
The ownership of precious metals, particularly gold, has become as much of a controversy as the issue of whether to buy whole life or term insurance. What has created the controversy in precious metals is the radical movement that believes the economy will collapse and gold will be the salvation of all wealth. While the excessive debt burden in this country could quite possibly bring about such a collapse, I believe that there is simply too little gold available and too much currency in circulation for gold to become the principal means of doing business. In my opinion it is more probable that the whole world's exchange system will become

totally electronic, using no currency at all. At that point, gold will become just another speculative commodity. So I recommend limiting any investment in precious metals to around 5 percent and certainly no more than 15 percent, of your total investment funds.

The price of both gold and silver fluctuates wildly. When the demand for precious metals is waning, it seems that gold salespeople use the fear mentality to promote gold as the panacea for all economic woes. But remember that in most instances the metal is being marketed at retail price. And when you attempt to resell it, you may be asked to accept only wholesale price.

An alternative method of buying metals is through a discount broker. Discount brokers advertise in most investment magazines, as well as *The Wall Street Journal.* They will usually sell gold and silver for the current "ask" price quoted on the exchange, plus a nominal commission. Be sure if you buy through a discount broker that you take physical delivery of the metal. I have known several investors who opted to allow the broker to warehouse their purchase. Later, when they tried to recover their investment, they discovered the broker had closed shop and disappeared, along with their gold or silver. If you need to store the metal, use a bonded, established warehouse.

8

Retirement and Social Security

S ome people seem obsessed with retirement planning. They may even divert funds from God's work and their families and live like misers most of their lives in order to "retire in comfort."

Other people act as if they will remain young and highly employable for the rest of their lives. With few exceptions, this attitude is very naive. Often they will end up living on inadequate income, mostly Social Security, or being totally dependent on their children.

In searching for biblical principles of retirement I found there were very few references on the subject. In fact there is only one direct reference, and it is found in Numbers 8:25, "But at the age of 50 years they [the Levites] shall retire from service in the work and not work any more." Exactly why a temple priest was required to retire at 50 years of age, or what he did from that point on, is not clear. Taking the totality of Scripture in context we can assume that he had other duties to perform.

I interpret two fundamental points about retirement from God's Word. First, we focus too much on ceasing our work at too early an age. Second, since most of us will not have the same income earning ability at 65 or 70, we need to lay aside some surpluses in our higher income years for use at a later time. Proverbs 6:6-8 describes the prudence of planning for the lean years. And Proverbs 21:20 tells us that a prudent man stores some of what he accumulates.

I believe the best retirement investment that anyone can make is to pay his or her home off as soon as possible. As noted earlier, with rare exception it is better to use the potential surplus funds that would go into a retirement account to pay off your home mortgage first, and then use the payments that you were making on the mortgage to start a retirement account.

I understand all the arguments about the money in a qualified retirement account being tax deferred, and the interest on a home mortgage being tax deductible. Even so, paying off your home mortgage first still makes more economic sense.

The additional benefit of knowing that your home belongs to you and not some mortgage company is worth it even if it costs more. If you don't believe that, just ask anyone who lost his home in a bad economy. I know hundreds of families who have paid off their homes in lieu of beginning an early retirement plan. Not one that I have ever talked to regretted it.

Another conviction of mine, having observed many families, is that most retirement plans should begin at about age 40. Sooner than that and the average investor sacrifices basic needs. I also doubt that anyone has the insight to look more than 30 years ahead in our current economy and accurately project what will be needed at retirement. But on the other hand, waiting to start a retirement program much beyond 40 usually requires too much risk to meet even reasonable goals.

Without a doubt the vast majority of professionals who have retirement plans would be better off if they simply parked their money in low-risk investments, rather than aim for the highest return. It's that same old basic principle: If you can generate the money to meet your goals, why take risks trying to multiply it?

The fundamental principle in any long-range financial planning is to develop a strategy that will meet your goals and stick to it. To do so successfully requires that some critical factors such as personality, age, and income be factored into your planning.

SOCIAL SECURITY

To supplement the following brief discussion of Social Security, you may want to obtain more details on the Federal Insurance Contributions Act (FICA). The most thorough discussion I have read on this topic is *The Complete and Easy Guide to Social Security and Medicare* by Faustin Jehle (Fraser Inc.).

I decided to include a separate section on Social Security retirement benefits because, like it or not, for the majority of Americans it is a forced "old age pension plan" that requires a substantial contribution from the day most of us go to work until we retire — or die. At present all covered workers are required to "contribute" over 15½ percent of their wages up to $53,400 a year. It is an absolute certainty that both the percentage and the maximum salary to be taxed will increase during the next decade as more "baby boomers" retire.

Many salaried employees do not realize that the total FICA tax is over 15 percent because the portion an employee must pay is one-half of the total tax. But I assure you that the portion paid by an employer is a part of an employee's salary, and directly affects what an employer can pay in total salary.

Social Security does have some good benefits, especially for those people who would never discipline themselves to put anything aside for later years. But actually it is a bad investment, as far as retirement benefits go. For someone who began working in 1960 at age 25, and paid into the system for the next 42 years until age 67 (the retirement age for workers born since 1938), the contributions they made to Social Security (assuming they started at the 50 percent of maximum level and went to 100 percent in 10 years) would yield a retirement income of approximately $20,000 a year. The same amount of investment in an annuity that earned 6 percent (tax deferred) would pay over $60,000 a year at age 67! And the income from the

125

annuity would not be affected by additional outside earnings, as Social Security benefits are.

But since contributions to the system are no longer "voluntary," you do need to understand how the system functions and what you can expect to receive at retirement age. For those workers born before 1938, the retirement age is 65 for 100 percent benefits. Social Security offers the option to retire as early as age 62 (disabled workers are subject to more lenient rules). Those who elect to retire at age 62 have their retirement benefits reduced by 20 percent.

If you retire at any time before age 65, your benefits are reduced by 0.555 times the number of months before retirement age. For instance, if you retire 30 months early, your formula would be 30 x 0.555 = 16.65%; so your benefits would be reduced by 16.65 percent a year.

To take a 20 percent reduction in lifetime benefits by retiring at 62 may sound like a bad option. But since you would receive 36 monthly checks prior to 65, it would take nearly 12 years of earnings at the higher rate to break even. So in great part it depends on your long-range goals.

GET AN AUDIT

Since the earnings you make during your working career directly affect the amount you will earn upon retirement, it is important to calculate what your benefits will be for planning purposes. This is particularly true for those over age 50.

A worker is deemed to be fully "vested" or insured once he has paid into the system for 40 quarters, with some exceptions made for those who came into the system as a result of tax law changes passed in 1984. However, since the government never makes anything simple, there are several exceptions. A quarter for Social Security purposes is also any period in which a worker earns the required amount ($540 as of 1991). So if you were paid $2,160 for any month that year, you earned four quarters worth of credit ($540 x 4 = $2,160), but you cannot accumulate more than four quarters of Social Security benefits in a single year, no matter how much you earned.

The schedule for minimum annual earnings has been increased as the Social Security tax and benefits have increased, so earlier years require less earnings, later years more.

Also, retirement benefits are adjusted for different levels of earnings, so participation in later years can enhance earnings, while nonparticipation will reduce retirement earnings.

If the accuracy of the Social Security Administration equals that of other branches of the federal government, you can expect some errors in your records. Many people have been shocked to find out that their benefits have been miscalculated due to contributions not being allocated to their accounts properly. It is important to audit your Social Security file prior to retirement so that you can clear up any errors if necessary. The Social Security Administration will run a free audit of your file upon

Investing in Your Independent Years

SOCIAL SECURITY ADMINISTRATION

Request for Earnings and Benefit Estimate Statement

To receive a free statement of your earnings covered by Social Security and your estimated future benefits, all you need to do is fill out this form. Please print or type your answers. When you have completed the form, fold it and mail it to us.

1. Name shown on your Social Security card:

   First   Middle Initial   Last

2. Your Social Security number as shown on your card:

   ☐☐☐ - ☐☐ - ☐☐☐☐

3. Your date of birth: ___ ___ ___
   Month   Day   Year

4. Other Social Security numbers you have used:

   ☐☐☐ - ☐☐ - ☐☐☐☐
   ☐☐☐ - ☐☐ - ☐☐☐☐

5. Your Sex: ☐ Male   ☐ Female

6. Other names you have used (including a maiden name):

7. Show your actual earnings for last year and your estimated earnings for this year. Include only wages and/or net self-employment income covered by Social Security.

   A. Last year's actual earnings:

   $☐☐☐☐,☐☐☐.0 0
   Dollars only

   B. This year's estimated earnings:

   $☐☐☐☐,☐☐☐.0 0
   Dollars only

8. Show the age at which you plan to retire: ☐☐
   (Show only one age)

Form SSA-7004-SM-OP3 (9-91) Destroy Prior Editions

Figure 1

128

Form Approved
OMB No. 0960-0466 [ ] SP

9. Below, show the average yearly amount that you think you will earn between now and when you plan to retire. Your estimate of future earnings will be added to those earnings already on our records to give you the best possible estimate.

Enter a yearly average, not your total future lifetime earnings. Only show earnings covered by Social Security. Do not add cost-of-living, performance or scheduled pay increases or bonuses. The reason for this is that we estimate retirement benefits in today's dollars, but adjust them to account for average wage growth in the national economy.

However, if you expect to earn significantly more or less in the future due to promotions, job changes, part-time work, or an absence from the work force, enter the amount in today's dollars that most closely reflects your future average yearly earnings.

Most people should enter the same amount that they are earning now (the amount shown in 7B).

Your future average yearly earnings:

$ [ ][ ][ ] , [ ][ ][ ] . [0][0]
   Dollars only

10. Address where you want us to send the statement:

Name
_____

Street Address (Include Apt. No., P.O. Box, or Rural Route)
_____

City   State   Zip Code

I am asking for information about my own Social Security record or the record of a person I am authorized to represent. I understand that if I deliberately request information under false pretenses I may be guilty of a federal crime and could be fined and/or imprisoned. I authorize you to send the statement of earnings and benefit estimates to the person named in item 10 through a contractor.

▶
_____

Please sign your name (Do not print)

Date   (Area Code) Daytime Telephone No.

ABOUT THE PRIVACY ACT
Social Security is allowed to collect the facts on this form under Section 205 of the Social Security Act. We need them to quickly identify your record and prepare the earnings statement you asked us for. Giving us these facts is voluntary. However, without them we may not be able to give you an earnings and benefit estimate statement. Neither the Social Security Administration nor its contractor will use the information for any other purpose.

129

request. This form is the "Request for Earnings and Benefits Statement." You can obtain one at no cost by calling your local Social Security office and requesting a copy of Form SSA-7004SM [see Figure 1, pp. 128–29]. Once you fill this out and return it, the audit normally follows in six to eight weeks, and is called the "Personal Earnings and Benefit Record" (Form SSA-700PC).

After you receive the audit of your work record (and your spouse's too), you will need to review it carefully. It will show every year in which you were credited for contributions and how many credits you have earned. It will also provide an estimate of your projected retirement benefits (plus disability and survivor's benefits) and the amount by which your benefits would be reduced for early retirement [see Figure 2, pp. 132–33]. This is an excellent service provided by the Social Security Administration and you should take advantage of it.

By the way, a 1987 study done by the Government Accounting Office (GAO) estimated that as many as nine million American workers may have errors in their work records. So check it out! If you find that your file has errors, you will need to appeal to the Social Security Administration for correction. Finding the W-2s or similar records for past years may not be simple. If you have not kept them, you will need to appeal to the IRS for copies (good luck).

SURVIVOR BENEFITS

In doing your retirement planning it is important to factor in the survivor's benefits. I will assume for illustration purposes that the husband was fully insured for maximum benefits and chose to retire at age 65 (67 for those born after 1938). In the event the insured worker dies, the spouse is entitled to only 50 percent of his or her benefits (except in the case of disability or dependent children). Failure to compensate for this reduction can result in financial hardship for the spouse.

The best way to plan around this problem is to store enough assets to provide for you both with only 50 percent of Social Security benefits available. That way the transition will be painless for the surviving spouse. Since your source of income is unearned (as opposed to wages), the additional income will not affect your benefits (at least under the present laws).

Once your budget is established on 50 percent Social Security income, you can reinvest the additional Social Security as a hedge against inflation or premature death or you can give it to the Lord's work.

MEDICARE HEALTH BENEFITS

Perhaps the greatest current benefit of the Social Security program is health care for older Americans. I almost hesitate to comment on this feature because I am totally convinced that, except for retirees before the end of this century, the program will be greatly modified to eliminate many current benefits. Sadly, it is a great idea that is simply too expensive to survive long-term unless the government also goes into the health care business to control costs. And how would you like to go to a government hospital to qualify for Medicare benefits? One thing is

TABLE FOR ESTIMATING AMOUNTS OF SOCIAL SECURITY BENEFITS

Average Monthly Wage	Old-Age Benefit Age 65	Old-Age Benefit Age 62	Dependent Spouse Age 65	Dependent Spouse Age 62
$83	144	115	72	54
92	158	127	79	59
101	172	138	86	65
107	184	147	92	69
122	195	156	105	79
146	210	168	105	79
169	224	179	112	84
193	239	191	119	90
216	253	202	127	95
239	268	215	134	101
258	280	224	140	105
281	294	235	147	110
300	306	245	153	115
323	320	256	160	120
342	331	265	166	124
365	346	277	173	130
389	361	288	180	135

Average Monthly Wage	Old-Age Benefit Age 65	Old-Age Benefit Age 62	Dependent Spouse Age 65	Dependent Spouse Age 62
609	495	396	248	186
641	517	413	258	194
660	527	421	263	198
685	536	429	268	201
705	544	435	272	204
725	551	441	276	207
745	559	447	280	210
770	567	454	284	213
790	573	459	287	215
810	580	464	290	218
835	588	470	294	221
860	596	477	298	223
885	604	483	302	226
910	611	489	306	229
930	618	494	309	232
955	626	501	313	235
980	634	507	317	238

Average Monthly Wage	Old-Age Benefit Age 65	Old-Age Benefit Age 62	Dependent Spouse Age 65	Dependent Spouse Age 62
1250	710	568	355	266
1275	716	573	358	269
1300	722	578	361	271
1325	729	583	364	273
1350	735	588	367	276
1375	741	593	371	278
1400	747	597	373	280
1425	753	602	376	282
1450	759	607	379	285
1475	764	612	382	287
1500	770	616	385	289
1525	775	620	388	291
1550	781	625	390	293
1575	786	629	393	295
1600	792	635	396	297
1625	797	638	399	299
1650	803	642	401	301

Figure 2

TABLE FOR ESTIMATING AMOUNTS OF SOCIAL SECURITY BENEFITS

Average Monthly Wage	Old-Age Benefit Age 65	Old-Age Benefit Age 62	Dependent Spouse Age 65	Dependent Spouse Age 62
412	375	300	188	141
436	388	311	194	146
459	402	322	201	151
478	413	330	206	155
501	427	341	213	160
524	440	352	220	165
548	454	363	227	170
563	464	371	232	174
577	473	379	237	178
591	483	387	242	181

Average Monthly Wage	Old-Age Benefit Age 65	Old-Age Benefit Age 62	Dependent Spouse Age 65	Dependent Spouse Age 62
1000	640	512	320	240
1030	648	519	324	243
1050	654	523	327	245
1075	661	529	331	248
1100	669	535	334	251
1125	676	540	338	253
1150	683	546	341	256
1175	690	552	345	259
1200	696	557	348	261
1225	703	562	352	264

Average Monthly Wage	Old-Age Benefit Age 65	Old-Age Benefit Age 62	Dependent Spouse Age 65	Dependent Spouse Age 62
1675	808	647	404	303
1700	814	651	407	305
1725	819	655	410	307
1750	825	660	412	309
1775	830	664	415	311
1800	836	669	418	313
1825	841	673	421	315
1850	847	677	423	318
1875	852	682	426	320
1900	858	686	429	322

for sure, the morbidity rate would lower the number of Social Security retirees drastically!

It is my opinion that the trend in Medicare will be similar to that of the Medicaid program provided by the states. The Medicaid benefit is available by need only, and access to the system is limited to the indigent. If Medicare does evolve in this direction, the very planning that prudent investors do will work against them because it serves to build a strong asset base.

Assuming that Medicare does restructure to provide health care benefits only to the indigent, there is a possible alternative available. You can join with a group of similarly minded people of all ages who can provide the funds necessary to care for the older retirees. These are called "associations" and, in fact, there are at least two in operation now that I know of, and more that are sure to develop as health care costs escalate. The concept is simple and is based on the principle taught in 2 Corinthians 8:14-15:

> At this present time your abundance being a supply for their want, that their abundance also may become a supply for your want, that there may be equality; as it is written, "He who gathered much did not have too much, and he who gathered little had no lack."

Virtually every insurance company is founded upon this principle: that there are more healthy people than sick, and the healthy can pool their resources to care for the sick, knowing that when they are ill, others will do the same for them.

At the time of this writing the cost of an average family health care insurance plan is about $300 per month nationwide. The cost per family in these associations is only about $110 per month, primarily because the groups are comprised of nondrinkers and nonsmokers, and coverage is limited to major expenses related to hospital stays. Also, since each member has a vested interest in keeping costs down, there is an active effort to monitor and limit all excessive bills.

To my knowledge there is no other health care resource available that will provide as much coverage for so little cost. Normally even a Medicare supplement will cost that much, or more.

ESTATE INFORMATION

Since a portion of anyone's long-range financial planning must be balanced with the inevitability of death, it is important to plan for that eventuality as well. If you do no planning for what happens upon your death, the effects can be devastating on your survivors, especially your spouse. As stewards of the Lord's resources, it is not an option to ignore the inevitable. Indeed, it is the height of selfishness for a provider to ignore the needs of his or her dependents after death.

The minimum planning anyone should do is to have a current, valid will while living. A well-drafted will directs how the assets should be distributed upon the owner's death. Both husband and wife need wills in the event they are killed in a common accident. In larger estates, the tax consequences of estate assets passing from husband to wife to heirs in a concurrent death situation can severely dilute an estate. With no wills, the certainty is that the state is going to assume the worst case situation; that is, to their financial benefit.

A simple will (as of this writing) can cost as little as $100, depending on the attorney involved. The more complex the estate situation, the higher the costs can run. It is always important to locate the most knowledgeable attorney, even at a somewhat higher cost. The only time you need a will is after you die. If the attorney made a mistake, it's too late to correct it then.

ESTATE TAXES

The current federal estate tax law allows for an unlimited amount of assets to be passed along to a surviving spouse, and approximately $600,000 to other heirs, without incurring any federal estate tax. In larger estates it is important that the ownership and assignment of assets be carefully checked by someone knowledgeable in estate planning. For instance, insurance proceeds that are assigned to a surviving spouse as beneficiary become taxable estate assets upon the death of the second spouse. If the insurance is assigned to a trust with the surviving spouse receiving lifetime income benefits, the tax consequences can be greatly reduced.

The federal estate taxes begin (presently) at 37 percent on estates above $600,000 and go to 55 percent [see Figure 3, p. 137], so they are not inconsequential for larger estates. It would be a shame to allow your

Unified Rate Schedule for Estates and Gift Taxes			
If the Amount Is		Tentative Tax Is	On Excess Amount Over
Over This	But Not Over		
$ 0	$ 10,000	0 plus 18%	$ 0
10,000	20,000	1,800 plus 20%	10,000
20,000	40,000	3,800 plus 22%	20,000
40,000	60,000	8,200 plus 24%	40,000
60,000	80,000	13,000 plus 26%	60,000
80,000	100,000	18,200 plus 28%	80,000
100,000	150,000	23,800 plus 30%	100,000
150,000	250,000	38,800 plus 32%	150,000
250,000	500,000	70,800 plus 34%	250,000
500,000	750,000	155,800 plus 37%	500,000
750,000	1,000,000	248,300 plus 39%	750,000
1,000,000	1,250,000	345,800 plus 41%	1,000,000
1,250,000	1,500,000	448,300 plus 43%	1,250,000
1,500,000	2,000,000	555,800 plus 45%	1,500,000
2,000,000	2,500,000	780,800 plus 49%	2,000,000
2,500,000	3,000,000	1,025,800 plus 53%	2,500,000
3,000,000	10,000,000	1,290,800 plus 55%	3,000,000
10,000,000	21,040,000	5,140,800 plus 60%	10,000,000
21,040,000	. . . .	11,764,800 plus 55%	21,040,000

Figure 3

137

hard-earned assets to be allocated to the government when, with a simple will or trust, they could go into God's work.

STATE DEATH TAXES

Most states use the federal estate tax codes as their guide for state death taxes, but not all. These exceptions can be disastrous if you don't know about them. Figure 4 (p. 139) shows the taxes per state as of this writing. Obviously these can and do change if state laws change. I would heartily encourage you to contact a good estate planning attorney to verify the tax consequences in your state.

PROBATE COSTS

A number of books currently give much attention to how to avoid probate costs. This in turn has sparked an interest in the use of trusts to avoid these costs. Many valid reasons exist why someone would need a trust but, in most instances, probate is not one of them.

In most states the cost of probating (proving) an in-state will is nominal. I live in Georgia, where the probate cost is about $50. A trust to avoid this expense would cost significantly more, and the ownership of all assets must also be changed to assign them to the trust. I am not trying to discourage anyone from using a trust if their attorney advises, but be certain of the costs and savings first. Obviously the probate cost in some states is more significant. In fact, many elderly people move from high-cost states to those with lower costs just to

State	Death tax ($) On $600,000 estate left to: Spouse	Child
Alabama	None	None
Arizona	None	None
Arkansas	None	None
California	None	None
Colorado	None	None
Connecticut	$0	$37,875
Delaware	0	31,250
Dist. of Columbia	None	None
Florida	None	None
Georgia	None	None
Hawaii	None	None
Idaho	None	None
Illinois	None	None
Indiana	0	24,950
Iowa	0	39,825
Kansas	0	21,750
Kentucky	0	45,370

State	Death tax ($) On $600,000 estate left to: Spouse	Child
Louisiana	$17,050	$17,050
Maine	None	None
Maryland	6,000	6,000
Massachusetts	23,500	55,500
Michigan	0	33,700
Minnesota	None	None
Mississippi	0	1,400
Missouri	None	None
Montana	0	0
Nebraska	0	5,850
Nevada	None	None
New Hampshire	0	0
New Jersey	0	0
New Mexico	None	None
New York	25,500	25,500
North Carolina	0	7,000
North Dakota	None	None

State	Death tax ($) On $600,000 estate left to: Spouse	Child
Ohio	$2,100	$30,100
Oklahoma	0	17,725
Oregon	None	None
Pennsylvania	36,000	36,000
Rhode Island	7,900	12,400
South Carolina	0	33,000
South Dakota	0	41,250
Tennessee	0	0
Texas	None	None
Utah	None	None
Vermont	None	None
Virginia	None	None
Washington	None	None
West Virginia	None	None
Wisconsin	0	56,250
Wyoming	None	None

Figure 4

spare their estate the expense. Check with the court of the ordinary in your community to determine the probate costs in your state.

THE USE OF TRUSTS

There are two basic types of trusts: living (inter vivos) and dead (testamentary). These can be further divided into two additional categories: revocable and irrevocable. The first you can change while you are still living. The second you cannot. Obviously a living, revocable trust becomes a testamentary, irrevocable trust upon the death of the person involved.

Assets assigned to a living, revocable trust are still a part of the owner's estate, and the assets assigned to that trust will be subject to estate and death taxes, but not probate costs.

Assets placed in an irrevocable trust are no longer a part of the grantor's (owner's) estate and can avoid estate taxes if the trust is qualified. Obviously they would also avoid probate, since a trust does not require probating.

A testamentary trust is one created by the death of the grantor, usually within a will. The assets are assigned to the trust upon the completion of probate and the trust controls the assets from that point on. It is common for one spouse to create a trust within the couple's will that will provide for the care of the other spouse during his or her lifetime, with the assets going elsewhere upon the death of the surviving spouse. By doing so, a portion of the estate and death taxes can be avoided.

OTHER TRUSTS

There is a proliferation of other specialized trusts at the disposal of qualified estate-planning attorneys. Among them are many charitable trusts that provide current tax-saving benefits and allow the ultimate disposition of the assets to go to the qualified charity of your choice. I have known many Christians who have used charitable trusts to provide for their loved ones, save taxes, and fund the Lord's work.

QUESTIONS AND ANSWERS

Because of the many questions raised by such a brief discussion of such a complex subject, I thought that a short question-and-answer section would help to clarify some of them. I would always add this disclaimer: I am not an attorney, nor an estate planner. Before acting on any of the information in this section, consult with your own attorney.

Question 1: *Can I draft my own will without having to pay an attorney?*
Answer: Yes, you can in the majority of states. A self-drawn will is called a holographic will. Holographic means that it is a document written totally in the handwriting of the person drafting it. The rules governing holographic wills vary by state, and you must thoroughly understand the laws of your state to ensure your will is probatable (provable) in court.

Question 2: *What if one of my witnesses has died?*

Answer: In order for a will to be probated, the judge may require the will to be verified. If you used only two witnesses and the state requires a minimum of two, both must be alive and available. It is always best to use three or even four witnesses whom you know well. If fewer than the required minimum are still alive, you will need to amend your will with a codicil to have other witnesses verify it.

Question 3: *Should I keep my will in a safety deposit box?*
Answer: If you do so, you need to be sure that someone else has access to the box. Since a safety deposit box cannot be opened except by court order, the process can be lengthy and expensive in the event of your death. If no one else knows about the box, it may never be recovered. I suggest that you name your spouse as an authorized signatory, as well as your attorney or accountant.

Question 4: *Do I need a new will if I change residences from one state to another?*
Answer: Possibly. You need to have an attorney in the new state review your will to ensure it conforms to that state's laws.

Question 5: *What if I own property in more than one state?*
Answer: Generally, your estate is governed by the state in which you reside at the time of your death. Thus a valid will drawn in your state can control the distribu-

tion of assets in another state, even if that state's laws are different.

Question 6: *Do I need a will if my wife and I hold all of our property in joint tenancy?*
Answer: Yes. Joint tenancy means that the surviving tenant or spouse owns the property upon the death of the other tenant, but if there are assets owned outside the joint properties, they would not be covered. In our generation this is common where there may be large settlements due to negligent deaths, such as an automobile accident.

Bear in mind also that some states tax joint property as if the deceased owned it outright, while others tax a proportionate interest in it. You will need to check with an attorney in your state to determine how jointly owned properties are taxed, if at all.

Also, if both of you are killed in a common accident, the last surviving tenant would be declared intestate (without a valid will). The estate would be subject to dual taxation and additional legal costs.

Question 7: *Who can I name as my estate executor?*
Answer: You can name anyone you desire to act as executor of your will and estate. That person's duties are to probate the will and distribute the assets accordingly. You may choose to name more than one person to serve as executor and should always name at least three alternates in the event that one cannot or will not serve.

Unless you stipulate otherwise, many states require an out-of-state executor to post a bond. Some require a bond equal to the value of the estate. Since your estate will have to bear this cost, you may want to waive the requirement to post bond.

Bear in mind that if you use a professional executor, a fee will be charged. This can vary from an hourly fee to a percentage of the estate value. Any such fees should be clearly spelled out in a contract and attached to your will or trust.

Question 8: *What is a trust?*
Answer: A trust is a legal contract to manage someone's assets before and/or after death. There are two basic types of trusts: a "living" trust, known as an inter vivos trust, and a "testamentary" trust, meaning that it commences upon the death of the person.

Question 9: *What is the advantage of a trust?*
Answer: A trust is not a public document, as is a will, and does not require probate. Thus, a trust ensures a greater measure of privacy. Also, since a trust is not probatable, there are no probate costs associated with assets held in a living trust. Since a testamentary trust is created within a will (normally), the will must first be probated before the trust becomes effective. A testamentary trust therefore does not avoid probate costs on the assets of the assignee.

If the living trust is irrevocable, the assets held in trust are not subject to estate taxes, except to the extent that the assignee retains an interest in them. Literally, the assets are given to trust and become trust property. There may be gift taxes due on assets assigned to a trust for the benefit of others.

Question 10: *Can I draft my own trust?*
Answer: Will and trust "kits" are available in most bookstores today. These purport to explain how to draft your own will or simple trust. While it is legal for a layman to draft such a "holographic" will or trust, I personally don't advise it. Once you are deceased, it's too late to change the will or trust if it doesn't pass the test. As the old saying goes, you can be "penny wise and pound foolish."

Question 11: *How much tax will my estate have to pay?*
Answer: That depends on the value of your estate at death. Through a marital deduction allowance, each spouse can leave the other an unlimited amount of assets. However, assets left to someone other than a spouse are subject to estate (death) taxes. (See the section on federal and state estate taxes earlier in this chapter.)

Question 12: *When are the taxes due?*
Answer: Usually within six months of death, the state will require an appraisal of the estate. The taxes are due and payable at that time although, in practice, both the state and federal tax collectors will normally work out a plan to convert the assets necessary to pay

the taxes so that the estate doesn't suffer a severe dilution through a forced sale.

Liquidity (cash) in an estate is very important since the taxes must be paid in cash. Otherwise, assets must be sold to satisfy the tax collectors. If the assets cannot be sold through normal market channels, the estate may be auctioned off at a substantial loss.

Question 13: *What if I change my mind after I make a will?*

Answer: You can change your will through the use of a codicil (supplement). The codicil is subject to the same laws of probate, so it is important that it be drafted properly. Attach all codicils to the original will and store them together. Remember that only the original will or codicil is probatable, so protect them carefully.

GLOSSARY

Annuity: A contract between a person and an insurance company in which the insurance company promises to pay monthly payments either immediately or at a point in the future.

Appreciation: A rise in value or price.

Blue Chip Stocks: Good quality stocks, divided into two categories by investment analysts: Growth (usually associated with newer companies or emerging technologies) and Income (selected because of their stable, long-term dividends).

Bond: A certificate of debt issued by a government or corporation guaranteeing payment of the original investment plus interest by a specified future date. Includes: church, corporate, current issue, junk, short-term, savings, utility.

Broker: One who acts as an agent for others in negotiating contracts, purchases, or sales, in return for a fee or commission.

Certificate of Deposit (CD): A deposit account issued by savings and loan associations, banks, and credit unions.

Commodities: The buying and selling of materials for future delivery.

Depreciation: An allowance made for a loss in value of property.

Deferment: Benefits or payments withheld until a future date.

Discount Brokers: Firms that place orders but not investment advice. You must know what stocks, bonds, or other investments you want. A small fee is charged for the service.

Federal Deposit Insurance Corp (FDIC): This agency, backed by the full faith and credit of the U.S. government, guarantees depositors of member banks coverage of up to $100,000 per account.

Government National Mortgage Assoc (GNMA): Called Ginnie Maes, the most popular of government agency securities, available in denominations of $25,000, guaranteed by the U.S. government, and subject to federal, state, and local taxes.

HMO: Health maintenance organization

Holographic Will: A self-drawn will written totally in the handwriting of the person drafting it.

Illiquid: Incapable of being converted into cash.

Intestate: Without having a valid will.

Inter vivos: Between living persons.

IRA: See Retirement Plans

Limited Partnership: A contractual arrangement specifying a general or managing partner and one or more nonmanaging or limited partners.

Mortgage: A contract to lend someone money to buy a home or other real property. The lender holds the mortgage rights to the property until the loan is totally repaid.

Money Funds: The pooled funds of many people used to purchase short-term securities. Not true savings accounts, but are short-term mutual funds that pay interest.

Money Market Deposit Account: Available at banks, savings and loans, and credit unions, normally paying a slightly higher rate of interest than a passbook savings account, insured by the FDIC.

Money Market Mutual Fund: In competition with money market deposit accounts, offered by investment companies. They are short term in nature and invest in jumbo CDs, commercial paper, or T-bills. Not insured by the government.

Mutual Funds: Offered by investment companies who pool many people's money to invest in securities. There are over 3,000 funds to choose from. There are "loaded" funds (meaning that the sales commissions and administrative fees are deducted from the purchase price up front) and "no-load" funds (meaning that no commissions or fees are deducted up front).

Numismatic Coins: Coins which are collectible and appreciate over a period of time.

Phantom Income: When the IRS says you have taxable income from a tax shelter or other investment but you receive no cash from it with which to pay that tax, you have phantom income.

Prospectus: The document that offers a new issue of securities to the public, required under the Securities Act of 1933.

Recapture: When property is sold or foreclosed, some or all of the previous tax deferments become due and payable, and the forfeiture of any outstanding debt becomes "phantom" income.

Retirement Plans: (Tax-Deferred)

401 (k) Named after Section 401 (k) of the Internal Revenue Code, a salary reduction plan whereby an employee may make tax-deferred contributions. The employer may also participate by contributing a percentage. Total contributions are limited to the lesser of 25 percent of salary or $30,000 per year. Distributions prior to age 59½ may be penalized.

403 (b) Also referred to as a Tax Sheltered Annuity or a TSA. Named after Section 403 (b) of the Internal Revenue Code, these plans are available to employees of public school systems and religious, charitable, educational, scientific, and literary organizations. Contributions are made by salary reduction on a tax-deferred basis. Total contributions are limited to the lesser of 16⅔ percent of salary or $9,500. Distributions prior to age 59½ may be penalized.

IRA. Individual retirement accounts are available to everyone with earned income. The maximum contribution is $2,000 per year. There is also a provision for a nonworking spouse, which is limited to $250 per year. IRAs for single individuals are limited to those with adjusted gross incomes of $25,000 or less; married individuals, $40,000 or less; married individuals filing separately, $10,000 or less. Distributions prior to age 59½ may be penalized.

Keogh. A retirement plan for self-employed, unincorporated business owners, partners who own more than 10 percent of a partnership, and employees of either. Contributions are limited to 25 percent of earned income or 15 percent if it is a profit-sharing plan. Distributions prior to age 59½ may be penalized.

SEP-IRA. Simplified Employee Pension Plans can be employer or employee funded. Eligible businesses may be incorporated or unincorporated. Total contributions, including any employee contributions, are limited to the lesser of 15 percent of net income or $30,000. Distributions prior to age 59½ may be penalized.

Pension Plans. These are funded by and through the employer. Employees may be able to contribute under some circumstances. They are formal written plans that have defined rights, eligibility standards, and use predetermined formulas to calculate benefits.

Profit-Sharing Plans. Profit-sharing plans allow the employer the flexibility to contribute funds into the plan only when there are profits. Contributions are made tax deferred. Distributions prior to age 59½ may be subject to a penalty.

Stock: An investment in which you own shares of a corporation.

Stock Certificate: This provides physical evidence of stock ownership.

Stock Exchange: An organization registered under the

Securities Exchange Act of 1934 with physical facilities for buying and selling of securities in a two-way auction.

Straddle: An investment strategy involving the purchase of a call option and a put option, each with identical features, at the same time.

Surety: Taking on an obligation to pay for something without an absolutely certain way to pay for it.

Tax Shelter: Any investment used primarily to defer income taxes rather than for economic value.

Trust: A legal contract to manage someone's assets before and/or after death. Two basic types are Living (or inter vivos) and Testamentary, meaning it commences upon the death of that person.

U.S. Government Securities:

Series EE Savings Bonds. In face value denominations of $25 to $10,000, series EE bonds are issued at a discount and are redeemable at the face value at maturity; thus no actual interest is paid.

Series HH Savings Bonds. Sold at par and the interest is paid semi-annually. Denominations range from $500 to $10,000 and may be redeemed six months after the issue date.

Treasury Bills. T-bills are short term in nature. The maximum maturity is one year, the most common maturities are 91 and 182 days. Sold at a discount-to-face value, the minimum unit is $10,000. T-bills are direct obligations of the U.S. government.

Treasury Bonds. These have the longest maturities

of the treasuries with maturities of seven to twenty-five years. Like Treasury notes, they provide direct interest and are sold in denominations of $1,000 and higher. Treasury bonds are direct obligations of the U.S. government.

Treasury Notes. Intermediate term securities ranging from one to seven years. They provide direct interest and are sold in denominations of $1,000 and higher. Treasury notes are direct obligations of the U.S. government.

Christian
Financial
Concepts
Teaching God's Principles of Handling Money

Larry Burkett, founder and president of Christian Financial Concepts, is the best-selling author of more than a dozen books on business and personal finances. He also hosts two radio programs broadcast on hundreds of stations worldwide.

Larry holds degrees in marketing and finance, and for several years served as a manager in the space program at Cape Canaveral, Florida. He also has been vice president of an electronics manufacturing firm. Larry's education, business experience, and solid understanding of God's Word enable him to give practical, Bible-based financial counsel to families, churches, and businesses.

Founded in 1976, Christian Financial Concepts is a nonprofit, nondenominational ministry dedicated to helping God's people gain a clear understanding of how to manage their money according to scriptural principles. While practical assistance is provided on many levels, the purpose of CFC is simply *to bring glory to God by freeing His people from financial bondage so they may serve Him to their utmost.*

One major avenue of ministry involves the training of volunteers in budget and debt counseling and linking them with financially troubled families and individuals through a nationwide referral network. CFC also provides financial management seminars and workshops for churches and other groups. (Formats available include audio, video, video with moderator, and live instruction.) A full line of printed and audiovisual materials related to money management is available through CFC's materials department (1-800-722-1976).

Career Pathways, another outreach of Christian Financial Concepts, helps teenagers and adults find their occupational calling. The Career Pathways "Testing Package" gauges a person's work priorities, skills, vocational interests, and personality. Reports in each of these areas define a person's strengths, weaknesses, and unique, God-given pattern for work.

For further information about the ministry of Christian Financial Concepts, write to:

Christian Financial Concepts
P.O. Box 2377
Gainesville, Georgia 30503-2377